OXFORD STUDIES IN LANGUAGE CONTACT

Series Editors: Suzanne Romaine, Merton College, Oxford,
and Peter Mühlhäusler, Linacre College, Oxford

The Languages of Jerusalem

OXFORD STUDIES IN LANGUAGE CONTACT

Most of the world's speech communities are multilingual, and contact between languages is thus an important force in the everyday lives of most people. Studies of language contact should therefore form an integral part of work in theoretical, social, and historical linguistics. As yet, however, there are insufficient studies to permit typological generalization.

Oxford Studies in Language Contact will fill this gap by making available a collection of research monographs which present case-studies of language contact around the world. The series addresses language contact and its consequences in a broad interdisciplinary context which includes not only linguistics but also social, historical, cultural, and psychological perspectives. It will not only provide an indispensable source of data for the serious researcher, but will also contribute significantly to theoretical development in the field.

The Languages of Jerusalem

BERNARD SPOLSKY
and
ROBERT L. COOPER

CLARENDON PRESS · OXFORD
1991

Oxford University Press, Walton Street, Oxford OX2 6DP
Oxford New York Toronto
Delhi Bombay Calcutta Madras Karachi
Petaling Jaya Singapore Hong Kong Tokyo
Nairobi Dar es Salaam Cape Town
Melbourne Auckland
and associated companies in
Berlin Ibadan

Oxford is a trade mark of Oxford University Press

Published in the United States
by Oxford University Press, New York

© Bernard Spolsky and Robert L. Cooper 1991

British Library Cataloguing in Publication Data
data available
ISBN 0-19-823908-4

Library of Congress Cataloging in Publication Data
data available
ISBN 0-19-823908-4

Typeset by Hope Services (Abingdon) Ltd
Printed in Great Britain by
Biddles Ltd,
Guildford & King's Lynn

Pray for the peace of Jerusalem . . .

Psalms 122: 6.

Rabbi Jonathan of Bet Gubrin said, Four languages are of value: Greek for song, Latin for war, Aramaic for dirges, and Hebrew for speaking.

Jerusalem Talmud, Tractate Sotah 7: 2, 30*a*.

Preface

A CONVERSATION that we overheard a few years ago in a bus terminal prompted us to think about the central issue that has permeated our study of the socio-linguistics of the Old City of Jerusalem. Two young Israelis who seemed to be strangers to each other were talking; one was an orthodox Jew and the other a Muslim Arab. Their conversation, about religious beliefs, was being conducted in fluent colloquial Hebrew. The Jewish young man was arguing that the great monotheistic religions hold certain beliefs in common: these common beliefs are true, he said. But before completing the utterance, he asked his Arab interlocutor if the Arabic word he remembered for 'true' was the correct one; when he was assured that it was, he completed his statement using the Arabic term.

The socio-linguistic facts interested us, and we discussed them afterwards for a long time. The fact that the Israeli Arab had learned to speak Hebrew fluently, whereas the Israeli Jew had not learned the local variety of Arabic (he explained to us afterwards that he only spoke Mugrabi, the North African variety his parents had brought with them when they came to Israel from Morocco), highlighted the unequal power relations between speakers of the two official languages of Israel. However, in this conversation, the Jew's expression of regret at not knowing Palestinian Arabic, and his offering, as it were, of a word of Arabic appeared to be an attempt to mitigate the harshness of this situation. His use of an Arabic word in a Hebrew sentence seemed to him to strengthen the universalism of its content: in spite of differences of religion, he was saying, the two of them could agree on beliefs.

But using the first language of one's interlocutor is not always intended to be, nor is it always interpreted as, a friendly gesture. We later heard one account of an Israeli Jewish woman, a teacher of Arabic in an Israeli school, who addressed a shopkeeper in the Old City of Jerusalem in her fluent Arabic. 'Don't speak to me in Arabic,' he shouted; 'use your own language!' Her use of fluent (but Hebrew-accented) Arabic may well have struck the shopkeeper as an inappropriate claim for solidarity. Barriers between groups, it seems, can be maintained more easily if the key to contact is in the hands of the gatekeepers.

The complexity of the issue of language knowledge and related attitudes may be illustrated by two news stories that appeared on different pages of a Hebrew daily paper in March 1989. The first reported a recent study of the teaching of Arabic in Jewish schools by Dr Hezi Brosh of Tel Aviv University. The item headlined the investigator's belief that the learning was being blocked by strong feelings against Arabs: you cannot learn the language of your enemy, it seemed to suggest. On another page of the same paper there was a report about a unit of the Frontier Police being moved into the Gaza Strip. It, too, had a language point to its headline: the local inhabitants were quoted as saying that the soldiers in the Frontier Police (whether Jewish, Druse, or Bedouin) knew Arabic well and hated the Arab inhabitants of Gaza. Knowing the language of the enemy, it seemed to say, did not lead to any better attitudes. Clearly, simple models of the relation between language and society will not work.

Because of the close association between language use and social structure, the study of language use in a multilingual community is at the same time both a powerful and a delicate method of studying the dynamics of group interactions in such a society. Because language is a symbol expressing social attachments, aspirations, and values rather than just a method of communicating referential content, it provides clues to the social forces underlying contact among the groups. Language is not just the medium for the message; it is regularly part of the message itself.

The locus of our study of language knowledge and use has been within the walls of the Old City of Jerusalem. Because the Old City is small and densely populated, the Arabs and Jews who live within it are potentially in daily contact with each other. Furthermore, because it is both a magnet for pilgrimage and tourism and an important centre of retail trade for Jerusalem and the surrounding area, the residents of the Old City are able to interact with people from outside the community even without themselves venturing outside the gates. Thus, there are many opportunities for language contact among the groups living inside the Old City and between them and people from outside the walls. The walls of the Old City (both those that divide it from the outside and those that surround the courtyards and neighbourhoods inside) make it easier to recognize social boundaries. We were thus provided with a complex microcosm ready-made for study.

In the pages that follow we report on our research and its conclusions. The field study, which was supported by a grant from the Ford Foundation through the Israel Foundations for Research to Bar-Ilan University, was conducted between 1983 and 1986. We were assisted in the work by Muhammad Amara (Bar-Ilan University), Michael Hallel (Bar-Ilan University), Suheir Hani (Hebrew University), and Pnina Rosenblitt (Boyer School), whose contributions go well beyond the normal work of research assistants.

In the first chapter we outline the superficial socio-linguistic impression of the Old City, describe the approach to our study, summarize the overall results, and raise the fundamental questions to be considered in the rest of the volume. In the next four chapters we provide a historical background to our study: Chapter 2 discusses Jewish multilingualism from the period of the Second Temple until modern times; Chapters 3 and 4 contain a detailed exploration of the socio-linguistics of Jerusalem a hundred years ago; and Chapter 5 describes the revival of the Hebrew language and its spread. Turning to the present day, Chapter 6 deals in more detail with the signs described in the first chapter, and proposes a set of rules accounting for language choice in the signs. In Chapter 7 this model of language choice is further developed, being applied in particular to the use of languages observed in the market-place. Chapter 8 suggests the effects and limitations of formal intervention in the process of language planning. Chapter 9 deals with language learning, showing the way in which the social context has accounted for language knowledge and use. Chapter 10 deals with the issue of language spread, looking in particular at how Arabic-speaking Palestinians in the Old City have acquired Hebrew, resulting in a reversal of the language situation a hundred years ago. In Chapter 11 we present some conclusions.

The original study on which this book is based was carried out by both authors, who met regularly and participated equally in all stages of the work. The chapters of this book have been authored individually; the first person singular in Chapters 1, 2, 3, 4, 6, and 7 indicates Spolsky, and in Chapters 8 and 10 Cooper; but it has been edited and revised jointly, so that whenever we say 'we', we mean both of us. We consider the study and the book to be joint work, and share responsibility for the good and, if pressed, the bad.

Technical terms and words from Hebrew, Arabic, or other languages that we have felt it necessary to use are glossed when they first appear and again in the index.

As this book is being written, the Old City continues to be in the news, and the relations between the inhabitants are once again strained by questions of control of its holy places and residential areas. It is our fervent hope and prayer that channels of communication will remain open and that the languages of Jerusalem will be used not for strife but for peace.

B.S. and R.L.C.

Contents

List of Figures

List of Tables

1

The Socio-Linguistics of the Old City in the 1980s

ANYONE walking into the Old City through the Jaffa Gate is immediately struck by the multiliteracy proclaimed by the signs. Street signs in Hebrew, Arabic, and English, advertising placards in those and other languages, building plaques in any one or more of a dozen different languages, all make clear that the sign-writers have assumed that the passers-by can read many different languages. When the market is open, this impression of multilingualism is quickly reinforced by the babel of spoken tongues. Even listening casually, one can quickly identify a score of languages being used. The most common is Arabic; next come Hebrew and English; with other languages making up a fourth cluster. If you go into the small shops or the churches, mosques, or synagogues, the language fair continues; and anyone who is able to enter into the houses, as we were, will start to discover the full complexity of the language pattern, the complex socio-geographic distribution and functional allocation, to use Ferguson's (1959) term, of the many varieties. This complexity will be sketched in the present chapter, but before we start it will be useful to give a brief introduction to the site we have chosen to study.

Geography

The Old City of Jerusalem in the twentieth century is geographically defined by its walls, built by the Ottomans in the sixteenth century, which still separate it physically from the newer parts of the ever-growing city (see Fig. 1.1). The line of the walls includes the Temple Mount in the east, now under Muslim control; it excludes the original City of David (about 1000 BCE), now occupied by part of the village of Silwan in the south, and cuts Mount Zion in two. The western wall of the Old City is close to the line of the original Herodian wall (about 30 CE), and divides the Old City from the new Jewish city that arose in the nineteenth and twentieth centuries. The northern wall sets off the fourth side of the rough square, following a line that also dates from the Herodian period and that divides the Old City from the newer Arab central and suburban areas.

Access to the Old City is only through its gates, several of which are limited to pedestrian traffic. Vehicular access is quite restricted: one can drive through the Lion's Gate to the lower part of the Muslim quarter; through the New Gate to the

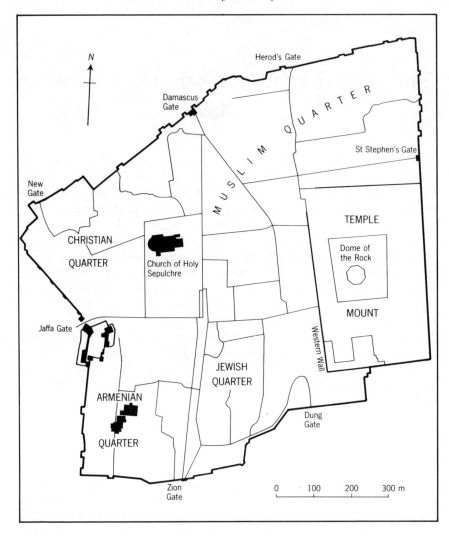

FIG. 1.1. *Jerusalem: The Old City*

Christian quarter; and through the Jaffa Gate around the walls past the Armenian quarter and the Jewish quarter to the Western Wall, with exits at the Zion Gate and the Dung Gate. A bus every twenty to thirty minutes serves the Jewish quarter; all other public transport starts and ends outside the gates of the City.

The few vehicular roads inside the Old City are narrow, and parking space is difficult to find. Most of the pedestrian thoroughfares are constricted and winding, the streets often going through tight, covered passages or descending flights of steps. Donkeys and mules, until a decade ago perhaps the most common means of transportation, are now rare; the main wheeled transport is provided by small hand-drawn carts; an occasional tractor pulls a garbage cart; and there is reputed to be a specially designed narrow fire-engine capable of penetrating the labyrinth.

The houses and other buildings rise two or three floors above the narrow streets, usually with discrete entrances leading to the courtyards on to which most houses open. To the pedestrian, the main impression is closed and claustrophobic; only a few open squares in the Jewish quarter or in front of churches in the Christian quarter, or the open space around the Temple Mount give any impression of airiness. But if you enter the houses and climb to the upper floors, the impression is very different, for you can see the life that is lived on open balconies and roof-tops.

The courtyards, though, do define life in the Old City. The term 'quarter' is somewhat misused in its claim to divide the city into four distinct areas; the Arabic term refers to a closed neighbourhood, a large number of houses clustered around a courtyard where, in the nineteenth century, there was a well and space for cooking. While the Old City is now considered to be unevenly divided into four quarters, named after the four major religious groups, the artificiality of this division is apparent. Several census cells in the Muslim quarter, for instance, have large Christian minorities; one of the cells in the Jewish quarter has a large Muslim minority; and the Armenian quarter census lines overlap those of the new Jewish quarter. That part of the Armenian quarter which is located inside the walls of the Armenian convent, with gates that close about 9.30 p.m. every night, is the paradigmatic 'closed quarter' (Azarya 1984), but life in much of the Old City reflects a similar, almost cloistered existence; after dark, most activity goes on inside the closed gates of the courtyards. The Jewish quarter is the exception, with young people sitting outside in the squares until late on summer nights, and students from a *yeshivah* (a college for advanced Talmud study) passing along the street on the way home from late learning sessions all year long.

Politically, the Old City is part of Jerusalem; it was incorporated into Israel after 1967, and is the responsibility of the Jerusalem city council. But there are several special features. First, much of the land (especially in the Muslim sections, but also including the Temple Mount and elsewhere) is under the control of the Waqf, the Muslim religious authority, or of the various land-owning churches. There is also religious control of many other areas; for example, the complex regulations enforcing the status quo *ante bellum* that has governed the holy places in Jerusalem since the Treaty of Paris in 1855 as reaffirmed in the Treaty of Vienna in 1878 (Cust 1929). Second, two governmental corporations have special powers and responsibilities for development and rebuilding, one in the Jewish quarter and another in the other areas of the city.

The recent unrest has not spared the Old City. The market now closes on most days at noon and there are other strike days as well, although many of the merchants stand outside their closed stores offering goods from the street or attempting to entice tourists to enter. Violent incidents—four street stabbings, the stoning of worshippers both on their way to and at the Western Wall, a deadly riot on the Temple Mount—have raised fears about safety, and the number of tourists and Israelis visiting from outside the quarters has been severely curtailed. As we write this, the High Court is considering a claim from a number of Jews seeking permission to reside in a building they have leased indirectly from the Greek Orthodox Patriarch, and we are digesting the report of a government commission of inquiry into the Temple Mount riot. Our study, however, was carried out some time before these incidents, and represents an earlier and, on the surface, more peaceful period.

This, then, is the area we chose to study: a closed but complex island (or even, set of islands) within a large city, with an intricate texture of history and present-day demography; an area where you are constantly reminded of historical depth (I live in a house that was built in the nineteenth century and rebuilt in 1979; part of the house is built over the Cardo, a Byzantine street with remains of Crusader shops, itself built over remains of Herodian and Maccabean walls); a city where the varied dress of the passers-by makes it hard to think of a fancy-dress costume that would not be current wear for someone in the neighbourhood; a city, in short, whose complexity is an obvious temptation to the socio-linguist.

Presumptions of literacy: Written signs in the Old City

When I first started to walk around the Old City, my interest was sparked by two signs, and they provide a useful introduction to the system of written signs in the Old City. The first was a carefully lettered sign in a shop-window in the main market, with the following text: 'ENGLISH, ARABIC & HEBREW NAMES IN GOLD & SILVER' (see Fig. 1.2). While the sign advertised the store's willingness to make silver or gold names in English, Arabic, or Hebrew (suggesting as a first interpretation that it was intended for people who read those three languages), the sign itself appeared only in one language; it was therefore reasonable to assume that it was intended to be read by people who know that language, namely, foreign tourists. The hint was fascinating: the monolingual sign offered multilingualism to the customer.

The second intriguing puzzle was set by a pair of signs a few yards apart on the same street (see Figs. 1.3 and 1.4). Each sign was written in three languages: the first line in Hebrew, the second in Arabic, and the third in English. The signs were square, made up of nine ceramic tiles cemented together; there was a decorative frieze or border all around. Two features, however, differentiated them. First, while the Hebrew and Arabic were identical on both signs, the English on one read 'EL-MALAK RD.', while on the second it read 'HA-MALAKH RD.'. The second difference, less noticeable to a literate person concentrating

FIG. 1.2. *'Names' sign*

attention on the writing, was that there was an extra frieze on the second separating the Hebrew from the Arabic. On closer inspection I realized that, on the second sign, the top line of three tiles, where the Hebrew was written, was in fact a later addition. In the case of the first sign, however, all nine tiles were put up at one time. The solution to the riddle became quickly evident; the first sign, with the words 'HA-MALAKH RD.', was planned to be in three languages, with Hebrew the first and main language; the English was therefore a transliteration of the Hebrew (the Hebrew definite article was used). The second sign was originally bilingual, in Arabic and English, with the English being a transliteration of the Arabic (the Arabic definite article was used); the Hebrew was added at a later stage.

My interpretation was confirmed when the picture was rounded out by another tiled street sign which I noticed on the Jaffa Gate (there is another example on a wall in Mamillah Road outside the Old City). This sign is also square, with a frieze border, and in three languages (see Fig. 1.5). But it is different in a number of ways from the two street signs I have been describing. The most obvious difference is the order of the languages; the first line is in English, with Arabic on the second and Hebrew on the third. There are other differences: the first line, 'JAFFA GATE', is English and not a transliteration of either of the other two languages; and the Arabic line is written in the elaborate calligraphy of Muslim

FIG. 1.3. *Ha-Malakh Road sign*

FIG. 1.4. *El-Malak Road sign*

art rather than, as is the case with the first sign, in a clear and legible modern Arabic script.

Having noticed all these facts, I was ready to propose that these three street signs provide a written record of the recent history of the Old City. The sign on the Jaffa Gate appears to date from the British Mandate period, which lasted from 1919 until 1948, which is why it is written in the three official languages of the Mandate government: English first; Arabic second; and Hebrew third. The use of calligraphic script for the Arabic suggests that the sign-writer did not assume that Arabs would actually need to read the sign. The second sign historically is the expanded sign, which has two versions, each from a different period. The last two lines originally formed a complete sign put up during the Jordanian period, between 1948 and 1967, when it was written in Arabic with an English transliteration. The Arabic script used was a clear, modern script, reflecting a growing literacy and recognition of functional use. After 1967, when the Old City came under Israeli rule, this bilingual sign was modified by adding an extra line with the Hebrew name of the street; the Hebrew was added on top, placing it first in order. Since then, whenever new signs are needed, they are

FIG. 1.5. *Jaffa Gate sign*

prepared in the same order of the three languages: Hebrew first; Arabic second; and English third,[1] the latter a transliteration of the Hebrew.[2]

My curiosity piqued by these signs, I set off with my camera to record as many as I could: trilingual, bilingual, and monolingual advertisements and signs on stores; warning notices; labels on buildings, commercial establishments, institutions, and homes; directions and information about hours; commemorative plaques; and graffiti. In a later chapter I will discuss in some detail the system that seems to underlie the choice of language on signs, exploring both a simple taxonomy and a more complex model. It is obvious, however, that the signs proclaim that this is an area where multilingualism is established, where three languages—Hebrew, Arabic, and English—are of major importance, and where the public use of other languages is normal and acceptable. The multiliteracy of the signs is matched by the multilingualism of the market-place, as the next section will describe.

The languages of the *shuk*

One way to characterize a city socio-linguistically is by the languages that its inhabitants know; another, by the languages its inhabitants claim to use. Both of these give portraits that are removed in some way from reality. The languages known, for instance, show the potential for use but do not necessarily show how much they *are* used; and the claims for language use are likely to be contaminated by the respondents' biases: what they report will be masked by their attitude to the languages. There is good reason, therefore, for the socio-linguist to want to gather objective evidence of actual language use. One fairly easy way of doing this is to observe the languages used on the streets, market-places, and other public places. The value of studying the market-place languages of a multilingual community has been plainly demonstrated by Cooper and Carpenter (1976) in a pioneering study of the languages used in twenty-three markets in Ethiopia, an obvious model for the present investigation.

The streets of the *shuk* (the market-place) constitute the main public place for the intercommunity contact in the Old City. There are no cinemas or other large places of public entertainment; places of worship are strictly internal to each community (although many are tourist sites); the many Muslim children who attend Christian schools comprise virtually the only intercommunity educational mixture; there is essentially no public transport within the walls (the exception is the bus from the Jewish quarter); dietary distinctions effectively discourage any social contact over a meal; residential areas are largely segregated; thus, contact

---

[1] As is discussed later, English has not been a *de jure* official language since 1948—only Hebrew and Arabic have that status by law—but it is *de facto*, and, as we shall see, it even appears alongside Hebrew on signs without any Arabic.

[2] We will discuss whether these signs are to be considered English or not in a later chapter.

between Arabs and Jews is generally restricted to the streets or to places of business.

The observed pattern of language use in the streets makes clear that the *shuk* of the Old City caters in large measure to non-residents, for while Arabs make up 80 per cent of the population resident within the walls, they constituted only 38 per cent of those who were observed engaged in transactions.[3] Moreover, while 88 per cent of the population claimed to know Arabic, that language was used in only 32 per cent of the transactions observed in the street, suggesting that some residents are modifying their language use for non-residents. This lends support to the conclusions reached by Cooper and Carpenter (1976) in Ethiopia, namely, that in the absence of a pidgin or special lingua franca, it is a common phenomenon in the market for the seller to accommodate to the language of the buyer.

While the general socio-linguistic situation in the Old City is quite different from that of the Ethiopian markets, it is interesting to note that the same general conclusions appear to be supported: rather than bringing about the development of a trade lingua franca, transactions in the market are sustained by the multilingualism of the sellers. If there is a language of wider communication, it is English, to which foreign tourists and local residents resort when they do not share a common language.

The socio-linguistic survey

The study of the signs and of the languages of the market-place may be considered as pilot studies revealing the multilingualism of the Old City. It was this small and complex sample of multilingualism that we chose to study in more detail. Our description of the language situation in the Old City is derived from a survey carried out over a period of seven months, with interviews conducted between November 1983 and June 1984. We were helped by four interviewers. Two of them, one male and one female, were what might now be characterized as Israeli Palestinians: both were Muslims and native speakers of Arabic, one coming from a town and the other from a village in the north of Israel; both were fluent in Hebrew and English as well, and both had MA degrees from Israeli universities; most of their interviews were carried out in Arabic. The other two interviewers were Israeli Jews, both native speakers of Hebrew and fluent in English, one male and one female, also with university degrees. The woman, born in Jerusalem and a long-time resident of the Old City, was fluent also in Yiddish and Arabic. All four interviewers were familiar with linguistics, three of them having taken graduate courses in socio-linguistics.

---

[3] The 1972 census reported a total population of 26,700 in the Old City: 17,900 Muslims, 7,900 Christians, and 900 Jews. The current Jewish population is around 3,000.

The interview schedule followed in the first survey was developed by the team and modified in the course of use. Most interviews took place in the respondent's house or at his or her place of work. Respondents were told that the purpose of the interview was to gather data about the knowledge and use of second languages; there were less than a dozen refusals to participate.

The interviewers were instructed to select homes or stores within a specified area, as defined by the 1983 cells for the census. The target was to interview 10 per cent of the households within each cell. There were no other attempts to obtain a stratified or representative sample, except that, in a few cases, the interviewers were asked to try to find a household speaking a language known to exist but not so far represented in the sample. In each household one person (generally the adult answering the door) was interviewed and was asked to give information about all the other people living in the house. The respondent was asked some additional questions about his or her own language use. Because most of the interviews took place during the day, two-thirds of the respondents were women. Readers should remember these facts, and note the bias that they introduced to our results: a tendency on the one hand to overstate linguistic diversity, and, on the other, to overstate female judgements about the language knowledge and use of their family members.

The survey contains data from 409 households, about one in ten of the total; the total sample population was 2,149 people, with an average household size of 5.25 persons. The sample selected was made up of representatives of the major religious groupings living in the Old City: over 60 per cent were Muslims, 21 per cent Christians (excluding Armenians), 14 per cent Jews, and 3 per cent Armenians. The average age of the sample was 25 and is slightly skewed to the young side.

The sample as a whole had an average of just under seven years of education. Major differences in educational level show up when the sample is categorized by religion. All of the Armenians and all of the Jews in the sample over the age of 16 had had at least an elementary education; and the Jews, although comprising only 14 per cent of the sample, constituted 42 per cent of those with post-secondary education. In terms of levels of education, the religious groups are led by the Jews, followed by the Armenians, the other Christians, and the Muslims, in that order. What is particularly noteworthy about the Muslim and Christian samples, however, is that there had been a recent marked improvement in educational level. This can be seen by comparing the correlations between age and years of education for each community. For the Jews the correlation was 0.71, for the Muslims it was only 0.05, and for the Christians and Armenians it was 0.09. Many of the older people in the Muslim and Christian samples had considerably less education than their children.

A good proportion of the sample was reported to be working: of those in the sample over the age of 16, 556 (43 per cent) were reported to be in the labour force. Of these, 74 per cent were male and 26 per cent female. When we look at categories of employment, the largest number was in the first two classes, academics and teachers (14 per cent of the sample over the age of 16); next came sales and services (10 per cent); semi- and unskilled workers (8 per cent); managers and clerks (6 per cent); and skilled and semi-skilled workers (4 per cent). There was considerable variation in occupation among the members of the four religious communities, indicating the unbalanced socio-economic distribution that accentuates the religious and social divisions among them. Relative to their proportion of the sample, there was greatest unemployment among the Muslims (23 per cent) and Christians (18 per cent), and least among Jews (3 per cent) and Armenians (2 per cent). A high proportion of Jewish women was employed outside the home. Jews were best represented in the three highest occupational classes (academics, teachers, managers); Armenians were best represented among teachers and clerical workers; Christians were strongly represented among teachers, services, and skilled workers; Muslims were best represented among sales and semi-skilled and unskilled workers. It is noteworthy, however, that students made up a similar percentage (about 12 per cent) of the Christian, Jewish, and Muslim samples, evidence of the major improvement in education among the Arabic-speaking communities since Jerusalem came under Israeli rule.

Claimed knowledge of languages in the Old City

In studying the socio-linguistic pattern of a community, a basic question to be asked is: who knows what languages? The question seems simple to start with, but a moment's reflection makes clear how complex it is and how hard it is to arrive at a straightforward answer. First, a person's knowledge of a language may be defined functionally (by describing his or her context-dependent skills in the language; for example, when bargaining in the market), structurally (by listing detailed knowledge of specific parts of the language), or globally (by attempting to obtain a reliable measure of overall proficiency). These various approaches tend to correlate substantially, but current language-testing theory shows that they are far from identical (see Spolsky 1989; Bachman 1990).

Second, the evidence of a person's knowledge can be gathered in a number of different ways: by observation, by self-report, and by testing (Spolsky 1989). Once again, there is likely to be high correlation among the results of these three approaches, but each suffers from its own kind of bias and error. Observation is limited both by the difficulty of finding opportunities to observe a full display of linguistic proficiency and by the presence of the observer (Labov 1972); testing has problems of sampling context and function, reliability, and lack of authenticity (Spolsky 1985); and self-report suffers from problems of unreliability and reporter's bias.

Third, there is even difficulty when it comes to clarifying what a speaker classifies as a language or what name he or she gives to it. The problem of language names is a complex one, and in the present study we were not sure, for instance, what was meant by a report of speaking 'Chaddic': did this refer to a local variety of Arabic or to a local vernacular language? Similarly, the exact language denoted by 'Scandinavian' is unknown.

Clearly, the theoretical need for exhaustive probing of a subject's language proficiency cannot be accomplished in a comparatively quick socio-linguistic survey. We soon decided to limit ourselves to the relatively simple matrix of language skills proposed by Cooper (1968) for the Jersey City study (Fishman, Cooper, and Ma 1971), and to aim to obtain global measures of ability in speaking and understanding, reading, and writing the languages named. We therefore asked about the mother tongue (first language learned) of the household member, and for a list of all the languages he or she could speak, read, or write. To give the respondent a clearer idea of what was meant by this request, and to add some minimal measure of uniformity to the answers, a more precise context was provided for each question. Thus, the interviewers did not simply ask which languages the household member could speak, read and write, but enquired about those in which he or she could carry on a normal conversation, read an adult newspaper, and write a simple letter.

As far as we can tell, these more precise indications helped respondents to form fairly accurate judgements of their own skills and of the skills of other members of their households. The results show, for instance, that babies and young children are regularly reported as not being able to carry on a conversation (although they are generally reported as having a mother tongue), and that schoolchildren are often reported as being able to write simple letters but not to read adult newspapers. One further check is provided by the fact that, later in the interview, respondents were asked to expand upon the actual use they made of the languages they had claimed to know; if anything, there seemed to be understatement rather than overstatement here, as a number of cases reported a limited use (e.g. shopping) of a language the respondents did not claim to speak.

It follows that, when we refer to language knowledge, we are relying upon respondents' claims of specified language ability either with regard to themselves or to some other member of the household. In other words, we are talking not of language knowledge in some absolute sense (if there were any way of assessing it), but of claimed or reported language knowledge. For the purposes of this study, we believe that these data, which are admittedly imprecise for any individual, add up to a reliable and valid overview of the socio-linguistic situation in hand, in much the same way as Fishman (1984) was able to demonstrate the very valuable perspectives to be derived from the even cruder data available from the language questions in the US census.

Monolinguals, bilinguals, and multilinguals

The general multilingual character of the Old City was made clear by the answers to the language-knowledge questions: close to half of the sample, of whatever age, was claimed to know at least one other language besides their mother tongue. Looking at the language knowledge of the sample as a whole, we find that about half were reported to be monolingual, a fifth to know two languages, and more than a quarter to know three or more languages.

The major language reported in the Old City was Arabic, claimed to be spoken by 88 per cent of those over the age of 5; second place was taken by English (45 per cent), and Hebrew came third (31 per cent); French was an important fourth (over 10 per cent), with Yiddish, Armenian, and German each accounting for about 4 per cent. The sample included speakers of Turkish, Spanish, Aramaic, Greek, Italian, Coptic, Amharic, and Romany. Altogether, twenty-five different languages were named.

The major language claimed as the mother tongue was Arabic, reported to be the mother tongue of 81 per cent of those in the sample over 5 years of age. The only other major reported mother tongue was Hebrew, claimed for 8 per cent of those over 5. Armenian was claimed as the mother tongue for nearly 3 per cent; French, Yiddish, Aramaic, and German each close to 1 per cent. Altogether, twenty-four different mother tongues were reported.

A quite different picture emerges from claims for second-language knowledge. English, with only 40 (2 per cent) claiming it as a mother tongue, was a second language for 839 (43 per cent), clearly establishing it as the principal second language of the Old City (see Webber 1979); Hebrew was a second language for 448 (23 per cent of those for whom it was not a mother tongue). Other principal second languages were French (233), Arabic (131), Yiddish (62), and German (53). After Arabic, English is the most useful language in the Old City, the language you are most likely to find someone able to speak, and the language most likely to be learned as a second language.

So far, the analyses have taken all three skills as being equivalent evidence of language knowledge. More information emerges by distinguishing between the skills of speaking, reading, and writing. Literacy skills are considerably below speaking skills. Thus, while nearly 90 per cent of the sample were claimed to be able to carry on a conversation in Arabic, only 60 per cent were reported to be able to read a newspaper or write a letter in it. Similar differences show up between speaking, reading, and writing English, Hebrew, and other languages. While reading and writing levels are more or less equivalent for Arabic and Hebrew, writing was claimed for a higher percentage of persons than reading in the case of other languages, and particularly so in the case of English. This reflects the fact that writing a simple letter (assumed to be achieved early in an educational programme) is less demanding than reading an adult newspaper (sometimes interpreted, perhaps, as actually being in the habit of so doing).

To sum up, half the population of the Old City appears to be at least bilingual; while for most of them bilingualism is limited to speaking ability, a good proportion is claimed to have functional reading or writing skills in more than one language.

The sources of language knowledge

Languages may either be gained as mother tongues or learned subsequently, formally or informally. Mother-tongue learning accounts for the overall pattern, and defines the Muslim and Christian communities as a whole as Arabic-speaking. It also clearly defines the Armenian community (a change, it seems, from the nineteenth century, when Arabic was the mother tongue of the small Armenian community) and the much smaller communities, such as Aramaic or Romany (Gypsy) speakers (of whom there were only a few in the survey). These smaller languages are likely to be known as second languages only as a result of intermarriage: you either are a mother-tongue speaker yourself, or you learn the language when you marry a mother-tongue speaker.

Mother-tongue learning does not define the Hebrew-speaking community, for only 62 per cent of Jews over the age of 5 were native speakers of Hebrew (in contrast, 97 per cent of the Muslims and Christians over 5 were native speakers of Arabic, and all of the Armenians were native speakers of Armenian). However, the vitality of Hebrew as the language of the Jews was attested to by the fact that 80 per cent of Jews under the age of 5 were reported to be native speakers of Hebrew. As we have already noted, mother-tongue learning accounted for only a tiny fraction of English speakers, nor was English known by very young children.

Among the Palestinian population, knowledge of Arabic resulted from the fact that it is a mother tongue; English was mainly related to formal learning, and Hebrew was mainly accounted for by informal learning. The Jewish population of the Old City had a comparatively high level of knowledge of languages (see Table 1.1), but the number of Jews who knew Arabic was not at all high, with just over 17 per cent of those over the age of 9 reported as being able to carry on a conversation in Arabic, and a bare handful reported as being literate in Arabic.

TABLE 1.1 *Knowledge of languages by religious groups*

	No.	No. of languages	
		Mean	SD
Muslims	1331	1.5	0.9
Christians	462	2.4	1.4
Jews	291	2.6	1.6
Armenians	59	4.0	1.3

Comparing the four quarters into which the Old City is roughly (and unevenly) divided, the large Muslim quarter is predominantly monolingual, although there are enough people, as we have seen, with knowledge of English, Hebrew,

French, and other languages to raise the mean number of languages known to 1.6. The Christian quarter and the Jewish quarter are on the average bilingual, with a slight edge for the Jewish quarter. The Armenian quarter (actually a mixed quarter, as mentioned earlier) averages out as trilingual. This becomes even clearer if we classify this knowledge of languages according to the four religious groups (Table 1.1): the Muslim figure drops slightly and the Christian and Jewish figures rise in proportion; even more dramatic is the fact that the Armenian community now appears as quadrilingual. When occupations were rated by need for intercommunal contact, the correlation between the number of languages known and the occupation held was 0.29 for all those over the age of 16.

These last facts suggest that what we are actually dealing with is a series of language islands (Kloss 1966), each one of which is contained within another. Within any specific island, monolingualism is only possible if the island is large enough; the smaller groups (the Armenians are the paradigm case) need other languages. Thus, the Jewish community is a Hebrew-speaking island within an Arabic-speaking world but with strong contacts to the English-speaking modern world beyond; the Muslim community is large enough to continue to resist in part the pull of the Hebrew community that has surrounded it, but it, too, is open to the English-speaking world beyond; and the traditional minority status of the Christians in the Old City increases their need for other languages.

The points of contact between the communities are education, work, and the street; the social life of family and friends is restricted to the immediate religious or ethnic community (or even sub-community). Street contact can be satisfied by smiles, gestures, and a few words. Education leads to formal language knowledge; the fact that the Jewish and Arab schools in the Old City do not place major emphasis on the teaching of the other community's language is a major stumbling-block to mutual language knowledge. The main driving-force for language learning, then, seems to be the instrumental needs of work; as a result, few Jews learn Arabic, and it is mainly those Arabs whose work brings them into contact with Jews who learn Hebrew.

Reported use of Hebrew and English by Arabs in the Old City

In the course of the first interview, after respondents had answered questions about the language knowledge of members of their household, they were asked to provide information about the frequency with which they themselves used the languages they knew, and the functions for which they used them. In this section we shall analyse the data concerning the frequency and nature of use of Hebrew and English as supplied by respondents who were Muslim or Christian native speakers of Arabic. The total size of this sample was 299.[4]

[4] The sub-sample is weighted to include those who actually know English and Hebrew, which is appropriate, as our interest is in their use of the languages. We must be careful not to assume that the results here apply proportionately to the whole population.

There was a big difference recorded between language knowledge and language use: quite large proportions acknowledged rare or occasional use of the languages, so that only 19 per cent reported speaking Hebrew at least once a month, compared to 31 per cent who claimed to know it; only 34 per cent reported speaking English at least once a month, compared to 53 per cent who claimed to know it. The rare or occasional users were therefore a very significant group.

The figures for daily use are also particularly revealing: 24 per cent of the respondents reported that they spoke English once a day; half as many made similar claims for Hebrew. Also, 20 per cent of the sample reported that they read English every day, and 17 per cent that they wrote it. For about a fifth of our sub-sample, then, English was clearly a most important second language. Reading and writing in Hebrew were much less common (only about 3 per cent of the sub-sample reported that they read or wrote Hebrew every day).

If we try to extrapolate from the sub-sample to the sample as a whole, we might estimate that while 18 per cent of the Arab-speaking population was claimed to know Hebrew, the group that used it daily was likely to be about 7 per cent. Similarly, while 34 per cent of the sample was claimed to know English, roughly half of that number (15 per cent) was likely to use it every day. Both of these are quite substantial proportions of the sample, confirming the multilingual nature of the situation; most of us have occasion to use our *foreign* languages only very occasionally; daily use is clearly the mark of a *second*-language situation.

While our question about the nature of use of a language was an open-ended one, the functions actually recorded fell easily into four main categories: use for work, for commerce (whether buying or selling), for education, and for social interaction. For both languages, the most commonly reported function for use was the first, with a fifth of the respondents reporting that they used English for work, and just under that fraction reporting similar use of Hebrew. It is possible to see this as corroborating the generalization that Hebrew is mainly a work-language for Arabs.

Hebrew was also particularly important for commerce (whether buying or selling); it was reported in this function by 15 per cent of the respondents, compared to 11 per cent for English. However, English was used twice as much as Hebrew (9 per cent compared to 5 per cent) for social purposes. English was also the dominant language in education: 13 per cent of the sample over the age of 14 reported using it in school or for other educational activities. In the case of Hebrew, only 3 per cent made such a claim.

We see, then, that English is used more often than Hebrew, but that this increased use comes from the fact that it serves a wider range of purposes: Hebrew is mainly restricted to work and commerce; English serves an equal share in these roles, but is also used for social purposes and education.

The inclusion of the other factors permits some other trends to be noted. It will be seen first that the frequency of speaking English is more closely related to reading and writing it than is the case with Hebrew. There were no significant differences in the frequency with which Christians and Muslims use Hebrew, but there was a significant difference between the two groups for use of English: Christians used English more often than Muslims did. Arabic literacy was more closely correlated with English literacy than with Hebrew (bearing out the educational connection), but both correlations were substantial.

Putting these together, we can say that those Arabs who read or wrote Hebrew were those few who were learning it at the moment, and their use of the language continued to be mainly concerned with the learning process. Those Arabs who had learned English to a high enough level in school continued to read it, but it was written mainly for education; a fair proportion, however, wrote English for work.

To sum up what emerges from this analysis: about 15 per cent of the Palestinian sample reported daily use of English for work, education, commerce, and social relations; a smaller proportion, about 7 per cent of the Arab sample, had reason to use Hebrew daily; this use was mainly accounted for by work and commerce, but for some it was also for present educational activities.

Our concern in this chapter has been to describe the knowledge and use of various languages by the population living within the walls of the Old City of Jerusalem. In the course of this description we have advanced some explanations, but a detailed analysis of the underlying forces governing the situation is the goal of the rest of this book. A first—obvious—source of explanation is history, and in the next four chapters a historical sketch will attempt to place the current situation in its diachronic perspective.

2

Jewish Multilingualism

In order to understand the present socio-linguistic situation of Jerusalem in its fullest historical context, it makes sense to start our study two millenniums ago, at the beginning of the first century of the Common Era. At least four languages appear to have played significant roles: Hebrew, Aramaic, Greek, and Latin. We will look at each in turn, and then consider the pattern of multilingualism involved.

Varieties of Hebrew

It is now generally agreed that the two varieties of Hebrew used by Jews in Palestine in the late Second Temple period are represented more or less by biblical and Mishnaic Hebrew. There are, of course, important distinctions to be made between poetic and non-poetic biblical Hebrew, and between early and late varieties, but for the purpose of this discussion I will treat biblical or classical Hebrew as a single type. Chomsky (1957), following Segal (1927), argues that Mishnaic Hebrew represents a later form of the vernacular spoken in biblical times. The differences between the two are easily and quickly summarized, and extend to grammar, vocabulary, and general style. Segal (1927) pointed out that the main differences in grammar concern the tenses, the expression of possession, and the dependent clause:

1. In classical Hebrew, as well as in other Semitic languages, there is no time-distinction expressed in the verb; tense differences refer to the completion of the action. Post-biblical or Mishnaic Hebrew has an established use of tense to signal time (see also Chomsky 1957: 162–3; Sharvit 1980).

2. In biblical Hebrew possession is expressed by the use of suffixes and by the construct case; Mishnaic Hebrew uses an independent word to indicate possession, just as we would use 'of' or a possessive pronoun (see also Chomsky 1957: 165).

3. Nominalized temporal phrases are replaced by temporal clauses (Chomsky 1957: 164).

Other changes had also taken place:

4. The use of the definite article in certain constructions had decreased (Chomsky 1957: 164).

5. Morphological simplification had occurred, with the dropping of the feminine plural forms of the imperfect (future) (Chomsky 1957: 164).

6. Verb repetition was no longer used for emphasis (Chomsky 1957: 165).

There were also differences in the area of vocabulary:

7. The meaning of a number of words had changed (Chomsky 1957: 165–6).

8. There were many new words added to the language, including some borrowed from Aramaic (Segal 1927: 8).

9. A number of words used in biblical Hebrew, especially words of a poetical nature, do not occur in the written records of Mishnaic Hebrew (Segal 1927: 10 f.).

While the differences between the two varieties are clear, there is some disagreement on their status in the late Second Temple period. In one view (e.g. Dubnow 1967; a similar view is expressed in the Talmud and is accepted by a large number of Christian scholars), Hebrew had become extinct as a spoken language some time after the return from the Babylonian Exile in 537 BCE, and had been completely replaced as a spoken language by a variety of Aramaic. According to this view, only the learned still knew and understood biblical Hebrew, which had to be translated into Aramaic for the masses. Mishnaic Hebrew was explained as an artificial language of scholars, developed by the rabbis in much the same way as medieval Christian scholars developed their own variety of Latin (Pfeiffer 1949: 379). So, it is important to start by considering whether or not Hebrew was still a spoken language at the beginning of the Common Era.

The argument that Hebrew died out immediately after the return of some of the exiles from Babylon depends largely on two references in the book of Nehemiah. In the first there are complaints about the fact that many of the Jews who stayed behind in Israel had intermarried with non-Jews, and that their children no longer spoke the 'language of Judah' (Hebrew) but 'half in the speech of Ashdod' (Nehemiah 13: 24). Nehemiah seems to have used Ashdod to refer to Philistines in general. The linguistic situation of Ashdod, which had also been conquered by the Babylonians, is not clear. Some scholars interpret his complaint as meaning that Hebrew had already been replaced by Aramaic, but it could equally well be considered a criticism of developing code-switching. In any case, it hardly supports the notion that the reason for the switch to Aramaic was the time spent in Aramaic-speaking Babylon, for it refers specifically to those Jews who had not gone into exile but who had mixed with the local people and with the populations moved into the area by the Babylonians.

The second text refers to reading the Torah aloud in public in the days of Ezra, after the return from the Babylonian Exile: 'And Ezra opened the book in the sight of all the people . . . and Yeshua . . . and the Levites caused the people to understand the Torah; and people stood in their places. So they read in the book, in the Torah of God, distinctly, and gave the sense, and caused them to understand the reading.' (Nehemiah 8: 5–8.) The Babylonian Talmud (Tractate Nedarim 37*b*) interprets the last verse of this passage as referring to the institution of the Targum, the practice when reading the Torah in public of following each Hebrew sentence with its Aramaic translation. It is possible that it refers to a translation into any language; it could also mean an interpretation given in more colloquial language. Fraade (1990) argues that, in fact, this passage relates to a single incident.

Even if the practice did not start as early as this, and even if, as Chomsky (1957) suggests, it was limited to neighbourhoods where the mixture of populations had led to Jews having a poorer knowledge of Hebrew, it is a fact that, within a few centuries, the Aramaic oral translation and interpretation of the written Hebrew Torah had become a firmly established custom of public readings. Fraade (1990) clarifies the distinction between formal and written versions of the Targum and the oral version accompanying the public Torah reading, and argues convincingly that it was intended for listeners who could also understand the Hebrew. The pattern of oral translation survived in some Jewish communities until modern times: Goitein (1971: 175 f.) describes how proud medieval Jewish parents were (at a time when Aramaic was no longer understood) of their children's ability to recite by rote the Targum accompanying the weekly Torah reading, and tells also of his meeting a Yemenite woman who criticized modern Israeli education for not keeping up this special training. But, as Chomsky (1957) and Fraade (1990) make clear, the Hebrew and Aramaic versions were kept distinct, and the Hebrew had the higher status. For some time the Aramaic version was considered to be Oral Law, which could not be written down (Spolsky 1986a).

These two texts and their later interpretations give some support, therefore, to those who argue for the early spread of Aramaic, but they are far from conclusive and do not themselves prove that Hebrew was no longer spoken. In fact, there is good evidence for the continuity of spoken Hebrew well beyond the destruction of the Second Temple, so that it appears to have survived for more than 700 years after the return from Babylon.

The case for Hebrew continuity has been presented by Hebrew language scholars, beginning with Graetz (1893) and Segal (1908, 1927), and by the Christian scholar Birkeland (1954), who argued that Jesus was undoubtedly fluent in Hebrew; most recently, it has been ably summarized by Rabin (1976). These scholars have demonstrated that the language in which the rabbis composed the Mishnah was not an artificial language of scholars, as, for instance, Pfeiffer (1949: 379) held, but just what would be expected if biblical Hebrew had continued to be spoken and to develop as a language. Its grammatical and lexical differences from biblical Hebrew are those of a living language, and not the attempts of scholars to reproduce an extinct language.

Further evidence for the continuity of Hebrew is provided by the fact, pointed out by Rabin (1976), that there were people who wrote in the style of biblical Hebrew until quite late. This was the case with the Dead Sea sects, who chose archaic biblical Hebrew as their written language even though their writing occasionally shows signs of contamination by the kind of contemporary Hebrew they, too, must have spoken (Rabin 1958). There is no reason to doubt, therefore, that the rabbis could have written in the archaic style had they wished; they had no need to create an artificial language. Furthermore, since the Mishnah was composed and transmitted orally and not in writing, there would have been no reason to have written it down later in Mishnaic Hebrew were it not as a record of the spoken version.[1]

Thus, the use of Mishnaic Hebrew in the Mishnah constitutes strong evidence that the rabbis of the period actually spoke Hebrew and did not limit its use to prayer and writing. Safrai (1975) argues further that Hebrew was the language of the Temple; most references in the Talmud to Temple life—sayings, prayers, blessings, readings—are in Hebrew, with comparatively few examples of Aramaic. There is also good evidence of the use of Hebrew by ordinary people. There is an account of the rabbis learning the meaning of an archaic term from a servant who came from a village in Judaea. Furthermore, a number of the Bar Kokhba letters (Benoit, Milik, and De Vauz 1961, letters 42–52) are written in Hebrew, in a style that is very similar to the Hebrew that is found in the Mishnah.

The distinction between the two varieties of Hebrew is, Chomsky (1957) points out, attested to in the Talmud; the varieties are referred to as *leshon Torah*, 'the language of the Torah', and *leshon hakhamim*, 'the language of the learned'; there are also references to *leshon bnei adam*, 'the language of ordinary people'. Some examples cited by Chomsky support his arguments for the nature of the distinction. Rabbi Assi, a third-century CE rabbi from Babylon, corrects Rabbi Johanan's use of the biblical plural *rehelim* (lambs) when instructing his son, and says that the Mishnaic *rehelot* should be used (Babylonian Talmud, Tractate Hullin 137*b*, cited by Chomsky 1957: 166). In another tractate of the Babylonian Talmud, Avoda Zara 58*b*, the Mishnaic term for mixing of wine, *mazaq*, is preferred to the biblical *masakh*. In a discussion of vows in Tractate Nedarim 49*a* the rabbis ask whether a term is to be interpreted in its biblical or vernacular meaning. Chomsky (1957: 167) argues further that the rabbis consider all three varieties to be included in *leshon hakodesh*, 'the holy language'; Aramaic is referred to separately as the language of the *targum* (translation) in Tractate Shabbat 115*a*.

Evidence for regional differences in Hebrew usage does exist: it would seem, however, that Hebrew was better maintained, or at least less influenced by Aramaic and other languages, in Judaea than in Galilee, an area where a great number of other peoples had been settled during the Babylonian Exile: 'The

---

[1] Gold (1987), in a review that discusses Spolsky (1985), takes up this point, noting the existence of later Jewish traditions of recording in one language (e.g. Hebrew) material that had been spoken in another (e.g. Yiddish). I am not unaware of the phenomenon, and mentioned it as a feature of Navajo biliteracy (see e.g. Spolsky and Holm 1971). The point here, however, is not that the rabbis used Hebrew, but that they used Mishnaic Hebrew; the argument is that Mishnaic Hebrew is evidence of the nature of spoken Hebrew. Further confirmation that the rabbis spoke this language is provided by the Talmudic rule that a tradition must be repeated in the exact words of the rabbi from whom it was learned. The rule is generally carefully followed, and there are many cases where there is switching from a Hebrew narrative to an Aramaic quotation, and vice versa. See Segal (1927: 19 f.); also Safrai (1975: 323).

Judeans who had been careful about their language succeeded in preserving the Torah, while the people of Galilee, who did not care for their language, did not preserve the Torah.' (Babylonian Talmud, Tractate Erubin 53*a*.) The Talmud goes on to discuss in considerable detail the kinds of mistakes that the people from Galilee made in their spoken Hebrew, complaining especially of the careless pronunciation which led to humorous misunderstandings. The linguist would recognize the kind of stereotypes often expressed about another dialect.

There is excellent reason to believe, then, that Hebrew was still a spoken language well into the first century, differing from the Hebrew of the Bible in those ways that one would expect in the normal course of development of a language with exposure to multilingualism. Fraade (1990) presents a strong case for continued Jewish Hebrew/Aramaic bilingualism in the Galilee well into the Talmudic period, during the third to sixth centuries.

How different, in fact, were the two varieties of Hebrew? I suspect, not enough to do more than slow down understanding: a speaker of colloquial Mishnaic Hebrew would have the same kind of difficulty with a text in biblical Hebrew as a speaker of colloquial modern English has with a formal written style or, at worst, with Shakespeare or the King James translation of the Bible. The basic grammar and vocabulary are close enough to allow for general comprehension, but further education is needed to make comprehension complete, and the written ability is even more restricted.

The other languages

Three other languages had significant places in the general pattern of language use in Palestine in the late Second Temple period.

Aramaic

Aramaic was one of the major languages of Jews in Palestine in the first century, and almost certainly the dominant language of wider communication. During the Babylonian Exile, as the book of Esther attests, knowledge of Hebrew had been maintained for some time, but the upper classes at least must have learned Aramaic. During Babylonian rule a policy of resettlement of conquered populations, reminiscent of the modern Soviet Union, brought a great number of foreign settlers into Palestine, and, just as this population mix has led in the Soviet Union to the spread and strengthening of Russian (Lewis 1972), so Aramaic developed first as the lingua franca between groups and then as the language to be used within the various communities. It is not clear, however, how fast Aramaic spread among the Jews who returned from Babylon or among those who had stayed behind. The earlier citations from Nehemiah reveal language diffusion and mixture, but not rapid language loss.

Aramaic was the principal language of the non-Jewish inhabitants of Palestine—the Nabateans, the Samaritans, the Idumaeans (the latter converted to Judaism by the Hasmoneans). By the first century Aramaic had moved from an imperial lingua franca to a local vernacular. It remained the official language for commercial and personal contracts, including marriage and divorce documents, and a number of Jewish books (part of Daniel, Tobit, Jubilees, Enoch, the Greek Esther, and the second book of Maccabees) were written in it in the first century BCE; others (Josephus' histories, Esdras, and Baruch) were composed in Aramaic in the first century CE. The virtual triumph of Aramaic is attested to in the second century CE, when, faced with the possibility of language loss, the rabbis started arguing for the need to teach Hebrew. By this time Aramaic was the first language of the Jewish home; Hebrew had started to become restricted to Jewish intellectual and religious life, although there is evidence to suggest bilingualism in Hebrew and Aramaic (and, indeed, multilingualism, with Greek as the third language) into the sixth century in Galilee (Fraade 1990).

Greek

The evidence for widespread knowledge of Greek has been presented by Lieberman (1942, 1950) and Hengel (1974). As early as 345 BCE Clearchus of Soli reports meeting a Greek-educated Palestinian Jew: 'He was a Greek not only in his language but also in his soul.' (Josephus, *Contra Apionem*, i, quoted by Hengel 1974: 59.) By 150 BCE a good knowledge of the Greek language could be expected of members of the Palestinian Jewish aristocracy; for instance, one learns in the first book of Maccabees (8: 17–23) that Judah and some of his supporters knew enough Greek to carry on diplomatic negotiations in Rome and Sparta. A young Jew who wanted to rise in the secular world would have to learn Greek; a good number of contemporary Jewish books were written in Greek. In the house of Rabbi Gamaliel, it is reported, as many students studied Greek culture as Hebrew.

But is Greek philosophy forbidden? Behold Rab Judah declared that Samuel said in the name of Rabban Simeon b. Gamaliel . . . there were a thousand pupils in my father's house; five hundred studied Torah and five hundred studied Greek wisdom. . . . It was different with the house of Rabban Gamaliel because they had close associations with the Government. (Babylonian Talmud, Tractate Sotah 49*b*.)

Even among the Dead Sea sects at Qumran, Hengel reports, there were many Greek papyri, and the 'Overseer of the Camp' was expected to know Greek. It was Lieberman who drew attention to how well the rabbis knew Greek. Not only are there many words in the Talmud derived from Greek sources, but at a number of places in the Babylonian Talmud—for example, Tractate Shabbat 31*b* and 63*b*, and Tractate Sanhedrin 76*b*—points are made with Hebrew/Greek puns of the kind that only a bilingual would be able to follow. The rabbis did not just know Greek but saw reasons to encourage people to learn and use it: 'Rabbi said: why use the Syrian [= Aramaic; also a pun on *sursi*, 'clipped'] language in Palestine? Either the Holy tongue or Greek ... (Babylonian Talmud, Tractate Sotah 49*b*). The relative value of Greek and the other languages is recognized in the Jerusalem Talmud, in a view attributed to the fourth-century Rabbi Jonathan of Beit Gubrin: 'Four languages are of value: Greek for song, Latin for war, Aramaic for dirges,[2] and Hebrew for speaking.' (Jerusalem Talmud, Tractate Sotah 7: 2, 30*a*.)

Greek was the language of the Greek colonies not only outside but also in Palestine; it was the language of cities like Caesarea, Ashkelon, Akko, Jaffa, Gadara, Philadelphia, and Beth-Shean (Scythopolis), just as it was of other Greek colonies throughout Asia Minor. Levine (1975), in a study of Caesarea, suggests that Greek was the predominant language of pagans, Jews, and, later, of Christians: it was, for instance, the language used on most Jewish funerary inscriptions. This was true in Jerusalem as well: Meyers and Strange (1981: 65) point out that two-thirds of the ossuary inscriptions found on the Mount of Olives dating from the first centuries BCE and CE were written in Greek alone; a quarter were in Hebrew or Aramaic. By this time it had also become the first (and, in many cases, the only) language of the extensive Jewish communities in Egypt.

Jews in Egypt had spoken Aramaic until the middle of the second century BCE, but, as Tcherikover and Fuks (1957: 30) show, Greek eventually became the language of intercourse in the cities; the Jews did not feel any particular loyalty to Aramaic, and it was quite soon replaced by Greek. By the time of Philo (*c*20 BCE– 50 CE) Hebrew was virtually unknown in Egypt. It was presumably for the sake of these Greek-speaking monolingual Egyptian Jews that the rabbis gave permission, recorded in Tosefta Megillah (IV. 3), for prayers in the foreigners' synagogue in Jerusalem to be recited in Greek.

It must be conceded that there was, at various times, opposition to Greek. Feldman (1987) argues, in fact, that Palestinian Jews resisted Hellenization; he points to the poor quality of the Greek on Jewish ossuaries, and believes that Josephus' knowledge of the language was an exception. After the tragic war against Quietus (116 CE) there was even a ban on the teaching (but not the use) of the Greek language, this being explained by the story of a Greek-speaking Jew who had betrayed Jerusalem to the Romans (Babylonian Talmud, Tractate Sotah 49*b*). But there is good evidence that not just aristocrats with close relations with the government, but also the rabbis, except for those who had come from Babylon, knew and spoke Greek. And just as with their use of Hebrew, there is no reason to suggest that the rabbis were exceptional in their knowledge of Greek.

Greek, then, had a role not just as the language for intercourse with the government, and for those Jews who lived in, or traded with, the many Greek towns, but also for contact with Jewish pilgrims from Greek-speaking Asia Minor

---

[2] Fraade (1990) draws attention to Palestinian Aramaic poetry recently discovered in the Cairo Genizah which demonstrates this use.

and Egypt. In the Greek towns Jewish knowledge of colloquial Greek was good; there is evidence in the Jerusalem Talmud (Tractate Sotah 7: 1, 29*a*) that the Jews of Caesarea said prayers in Greek; and Lieberman (1942: 32 ff.) reports a case of Greek being used in a street prayer there during a drought (it was customary to ask the common people to pray in their own language in the streets). He also points out that the rabbis often quote or refer to Greek proverbs in their sermons without translating, apparently assuming that they would be familiar to their listeners. A number of multilingual synagogue inscriptions, dating as late as the sixth century CE, suggest the continued importance and knowledge of Greek, Hebrew, and Aramaic (Fraade 1990).

Latin

The place of Latin is somewhat more difficult to determine. It was the language of the Roman army and of officials (see e.g. Levine 1975); probably much of Roman government, even in the East, was conducted in Latin. In Egypt, as Kaimio (1979) has shown, there is strong evidence that Greek was used at lower levels of government, so that non-Romans would be most likely to have dealings with the government in that language. Katzoff (1980: 821) points out that the edicts issued by the prefects are all in Greek, with hardly any sign of translation from Latin, although the prefects themselves were usually native speakers of Latin; he argues, however, that the Egyptian evidence cannot be adduced to the rest of the Empire. So, while Latin was present in the Palestinian area, Meyers and Strange (1981: 65) believe that it did not gain 'a firm foothold' but remained 'the language of narrow specialist application'.

Putting all this together, the picture that emerges, then, is that, at least until the end of the Bar Kokhba revolt in 135 CE, the Jews of Palestine were multilingual, using Aramaic, Hebrew, and Greek for different purposes and in different parts of the country (Weinreich 1980: 59 ff.). Hebrew was used in the villages of Judaea until then, and continued for a while longer—perhaps as late as the sixth century CE, if one accepts Fraade (1990)—in the villages of Galilee where Jews settled after the Romans drove them out of Judaea; Greek was the language of many cities and towns; and Aramaic was the most common first language.

Table 2.1 provides a summary of the regional and class variations in language-use patterns. The order in which languages are mentioned in the right-hand column is significant, representing the probable frequency of use and level of proficiency. The functional separation is much more complex. According to the pattern proposed by Ferguson (1959) as being distinctive of what he called 'diglossia',[3] the functions form two groups: a set of H (or higher) functions, such

---

[3] Ferguson himself used the term 'diglossia' when these two sets of functions are expressed by related varieties of the same language, as with classical and vernacular Arabic, or Haitian Creole and French; Fishman extended it to include cases where the varieties were distinct, e.g. Spanish and English in the Puerto Rican community in New Jersey.

TABLE 2.1. *Language use in Palestine and by Jews elsewhere at the beginning of the Common Era*

Place	Language
Jews in the Diaspora	
Egypt, Rome, Asia Minor	Greek
Babylon	Aramaic and Hebrew
Non-Jews in Palestine	
Government officials	Greek and some Latin
Coastal cities (Greek colonies)	Greek
Elsewhere	Aramaic
Jews in Palestine	
Judaean villages	Hebrew, Aramaic
Galilee	Aramaic, Hebrew, Greek
Coastal cities	Greek, Aramaic, Hebrew
Jerusalem	
upper class	Greek, Aramaic, Hebrew
lower class	Aramaic, Hebrew, Greek

Source: Spolsky (1985).

as public life, formal writing, religion, high culture, and formal education; and a set of L (or lower) functions, such as home, neighbourhood, and work. In first-century Palestine certain functional allocations appear clear—Greek was the language for government, Hebrew for prayer and study, and Aramaic for trade—but the functional distribution is much more complex, being more than just the addition of one more language to the normal diglossic pattern. This becomes clearer if we look specifically at the use of the various languages for literacy functions (Spolsky 1983).

Languages for literacy

As mentioned above, Latin was an official language of government, attested in military and other official and public inscriptions. Greek was widely used in public and private inscriptions: there was a Greek sign in the Temple advising non-Jews of the penalty for entering the holy places; Greek was used on many Jewish tombs and on synagogue inscriptions. One of Bar Kokhba's letters to his captains was in Greek, so we may assume a degree of popular literacy in Greek. Even though Greek as a language of literacy did not have the same importance for Jews of Palestine as it did in the Diaspora, especially Egypt, its special status is in fact noted in the Talmud, for whereas some authorities held that the Bible could be written in any language (Mishnah Megillah 1. 8), Rabbi Simeon said that it could be written only in Hebrew or in Greek (Jerusalem Talmud, Tractate Megillah 1. 1).

Aramaic had long been established as the appropriate language for legal and commercial documents. Two tractates of the Talmud deal specifically with marriage contracts and divorce documents, both of which were to be written in Aramaic according to carefully prescribed formulas. But although the form of the documents was clearly laid down, the rabbis held the written document to be less reliable than the word of those witnesses who saw it being written down or signed. As a result, no special status was attached to the ability to write such documents. Given that Hebrew had been written in the square Aramaic letters since the return from the Babylonian Exile, anyone who could write a religious scroll in Hebrew could presumably write a marriage contract in Aramaic, and there is a reference in the Talmud to schools for scribes where a teacher might be heard dictating a model divorce bill to the class. But it was not clear that writing these Aramaic documents had a special status: in fact, the Talmud says that anyone could write such a document, including a woman or a minor, neither of whom could give evidence in a lawcourt. However, in contrast to this, it must be noted that, as stated above, a number of important literary works were written in Aramaic.

One other kind of document was written in Aramaic, the Targum or Aramaic translation or interpretation of the Bible. I have already mentioned that such an interpretation had to accompany all public readings of the Torah, but the Talmud held that the Targum was part of the Oral Law. As such, it was not supposed to be written down or read from a written text, but had to be delivered, one verse at a time, following the reading of the Hebrew verse, either from memory or extemporaneously (Babylonian Talmud, Tractate Soferim 39*b*). The Talmud is clear that the Holy Scriptures could be written down only in Hebrew and that public readings as part of worship could only take place from a Hebrew text. But there are references in the Talmud to at least one written Targum, and there were probably others. While such documents could not be used in statutory services, they had the sanctity of other sacred writings, and could, for instance, be carried out of a house on the Sabbath to save them from a fire (Babylonian Talmud, Tractate Shabbat 113*b*).

What we seem to have here, then, is a kind of casual attitude to writing (except of contracts) that is not uncommon in a diglossic situation. Ephemera (personal notes of any kind) and even private inscriptions may be written in any language; but the rules are much stricter for sacred material.

The major language for Jewish sacred texts was Hebrew. Sacred-text literacy functioned on two levels, that of the ordinary person and that of the scribe. The ordinary educated Jewish man was expected to be able to read a portion of the Written Law aloud, with correct cantillation, from an unpointed (vowelless) text, as part of public worship. There is evidence that some women, at least, had these skills. The scribe had a twofold task: first, to train young children in the skill of reading aloud and in the elementary level of interpretation of the sacred texts; and, second, to copy and maintain the accuracy of the written text. The copying was done letter by letter, not from dictation or memory but from a written model. During Temple times the task of copying the Holy Scriptures was attached to the Temple; by the first century there were families and schools of scribes. Some of them became rabbis; the ability to write a sacred text was classed, along with performing a circumcision and slaughtering animals in accordance with the religious laws, as a most desirable way for a rabbi to serve the public.

To sum up, the period was multiliterate as well as multilingual. In marked contrast to those situations where one finds a bilingual but monoliterate community, there was an established role for literacy in each of the languages, with Hebrew being used as the main language of the sacred written texts, Aramaic as the language for legal contracts and commerce, and Greek and Latin as the language of government and of many public and private inscriptions: letters and ephemera could be written in any language. Each literacy was maintained by specialists and had its own training system associated with it. Although these specialists had important roles, their status was not as high as that of scribes in earlier times, for the skills of reading and writing were becoming more widespread.

The overall pattern

This description of the socio-linguistic situation in Jewish Palestine confirms the presence of a significant number of monolinguals, or at least people with whom a multilingual Jew would share only one language. With Jews from Egypt or Asia Minor, or with Greek colonists, or with the Greek- and Latin-speaking government, Greek would be the language for communication. Greek might sometimes be useful with non-Jews of other backgrounds, but the large majority would probably be restricted to the use of Aramaic as a lingua franca. With a good number of Jews, presumably the old and the young, coming mainly from Judaea (and after the destruction of Judaea, from some Galilean and Golan villages), the language for communication would remain Hebrew. Thus, multilingual Jews living in Palestine in the first century who needed to interact with any of these named groups would have good reason to both maintain and use their ability in each of the three languages.

The Talmudic citation reproduced earlier (p. 24) hints at a topical division in its discussion of the suitability of various languages, but perhaps the clearest statements of topical preferences are the extensive debates in the Talmud on the language for writing the Holy Scriptures (mentioned above), and the language to be used for public readings from the Scriptures, for prayers (Babylonian Talmud, Tractate Berakhot 13*a*), and for citing the words of a teacher (ibid. 47*a*). Briefly, preference is always given to Hebrew, with a special provision that some things should always be quoted in the original (e.g. an Aramaic word used in the Bible, or a teaching from a rabbi).

Learning biblical Hebrew

How well was classical or biblical Hebrew known among the general Jewish population? Here, as with most attempts at historical socio-linguistics, it is difficult to reach firm conclusions; the evidence we have is interpretable (and interpreted) in quite different ways. Mention has already been made of the specialized knowledge and skills of the *sofer* or scribe. The assumption in much of the Talmud seems to be that, while most people would be able to sign their name, their writing would not be as neat as that of a scribe. The Babylonian Talmud (Tractate Baba Batra 163*a*) assumes that an ordinary person's signature would take up more space than a scribe would require to write a line. The widespread use of the Targum seems to imply an inferior knowledge of biblical Hebrew. But this is far from conclusive, for even in a congregation where all of those present can be assumed to understand the Bible reading, there is still room for interpretation and explanation.

Perhaps a clearer picture of assumed Hebrew knowledge might be obtained from the system of public prayer. The standard daily prayers were not written down until quite late (the first prayer-book dates from the ninth century CE), but the general form of prayers (and the specific wording of the end of each of the eighteen benedictions) was set by early Talmud times. To lead in public prayers, then, involved the ability to compose, within established formulas, the appropriate linking paragraphs. From the sixth century CE until the eleventh and beyond, during the period of the *paytanim* (composers and performers of Jewish liturgical poetry), this was a specially valued skill, inspiring the composition of an extensive literature of elaborate and complex religious poetry; but in earlier times it seemed to be a common ability. Similarly, the ability to read aloud from the Torah (with the required memorization of punctuation, vocalization, and melody) seems to have been prevalent, as it remains among Yemenite Jews to this day. In most other traditions the task has devolved on a single reader who is expected to prepare the weekly text. There is an intriguing statement in the Talmud to the effect that women should not be called on to read from the Torah in public, for this will be thought to suggest that the community does not have enough men capable of doing it.

All indications are that, apart from prayers and formal literary compositions, all normal discussion and teaching of religious matters took place in a spoken variety. The pattern is quite clear in the Talmud, which is essentially the record of several hundred years of teaching and debate. Quotations from the Bible are in biblical Hebrew; citations from Mishnaic teaching are in Mishnaic Hebrew; discussions in the Babylonian Talmud then take place in Aramaic. The Talmud considers it a virtue to quote a rabbi in his own words, and presumably in the language he spoke.

We have signs, therefore, of a respect for multilingualism (for spoken Hebrew as well as for the other languages). Admittedly, during the period when the vitality of Hebrew was threatened, there were attacks on the other languages: Aramaic was said to be unnecessary; Greek to be the language of those who collaborate with an alien persecuting government. But all of these varieties had their place. Just as Greek or Aramaic was acceptable for formal prayer, so the vernacular variety of Hebrew was respected and often preferred to the classical.

Changes in the socio-linguistic pattern

The pattern that has been described lasted 200 or 300 years; there is disagreement about how long spoken Hebrew survived the mass dislocations of the Roman crushing of the Bar Kokhba revolt. The special relation between a vernacular (L) and a classical (H) language survived the loss of spoken Hebrew, but there was a substitution in the case of the spoken or L variety. Judaeo-Aramaic replaced vernacular Hebrew in Babylon and in Palestine, and was itself later replaced by Judaeo-Arabic. Judaeo-Greek replaced vernacular Hebrew in Egypt and the rest of the Roman world, and was then replaced in Egypt by Arabic, and in the West by Judaeo-Romance and later Yiddish. Changes took place in the classical variety, too, as the written Aramaic of the Targum and Talmud joined Hebrew as part of *lashon kodesh*,[4] albeit with differently defined functions. For example, only a limited number of prayers are in Aramaic, but, on the other hand, Jewish marriage contracts and divorce documents are still written in that language.

A third major change cut across this pattern of internal languages: namely, the various functional roles of co-territorial languages. Sometimes these languages were restricted to intercourse with non-Jews; at other times they were indigenized and modified as Jewish languages serving a large number of internal functions other than those formal ones reserved for *lashon kodesh*; at other times again, they entered both roles. The study of the sociology of Jewish languages is essentially the tracing of this ever-changing but basically constant pattern.

Jewish multilingualism through the centuries

An Israeli-born friend of mine told me a story about her grandmother, who had been brought to Israel when she was too old to learn very much Hebrew. The

---

[4] In modern spoken Hebrew the term is usually pronounced this way, with Yiddish stress, rather than the more strictly correct *leshon hakodesh*. It will be used here to refer to the variety of pre-revival rabbinical Hebrew, including Aramaic words from the Talmud, that was (and, in some circles, still is) used in daily Jewish religious life.

grandmother always spoke Yiddish, but, one day, when an Arab came to the door selling vegetables, she was heard to address him in Russian. 'Why did you speak to the man in Russian?', she was asked. 'Oh', she replied in Yiddish, 'with Jews [*yidn*] you speak Yiddish, with non-Jews [*goyim*] you speak Goyish [Gentile].'[5] In this sentence she summed up one of the key points of Jewish multilingualism: a meaningful choice between a language for use within the community, and another for use outside it. The choice of language is itself the message: speaking Yiddish to someone proclaims a belief that he is an insider; speaking Goyish proclaims that he is an outsider. This may still be observed at the Western Wall when groups are being formed for afternoon prayers. A passer-by is first asked in Hebrew or in Yiddish, according to his appearance: 'Have you prayed yet?' If he fails to respond to the question in either of those languages, he is likely to be asked, in English: 'Are you Jewish?'

Aramaic was the first of a long line of what are now called Jewish languages, specifically Jewish varieties of co-territorial languages that have come to serve in the home and within the Jewish community as the language of normal life, and that are defined especially by their special relation to the language of Jewish classical texts. Understanding the process of the development of Jewish languages is important, for it exemplifies the special function of Jewish multilingualism in permitting a kind of acculturation that does not become assimilation. It starts when Jews in a minority situation, whether through numerical or political and economic weakness, come to adopt the majority and alien language, the co-territorial vernacular, not just as a language for communication with outsiders, but as the language for internal community functions.

It is important to stress how much this step threatens the identity of the community, for the universal adoption and internalization of another people's language brings with it the clear danger of assimilation of, and submersion in, its culture and life. How the process occurs has been suggested by Weinreich (1980). First, the alien language is employed only in dealings with members of the outside community; it remains 'Goyish'. For members of a minority group, the status of those with well-developed skills in dealing with the majority community is high; so high that they start to signal this status by using the alien language within the community itself. Breitborde (1983) provides an incisive analysis of this process in a Kroo–English bilingual community in Liberia, where younger preachers show their status by an expected use of English in their preaching and praying. From these first, limited internal uses, setting up high attitudinal value for the alien but majority language, it is a common step to move to more extensive internal use. The process is clearly exemplified in the case of many immigrants; a regular concomitant of migration is the weakening of internal values.

[5] We have heard another form of this story. During the British Mandate period an old Jewish woman from Safed moved to Jerusalem, where she was heard to address a British policeman in Arabic. 'What else', she said, 'do you speak to goyim?'

But there is the potential of protection against this, especially if there exists an internal language with high associated status—most obviously, when it is a language associated with religion or important religious texts or practices: sacred literacy serves to balance the pull towards the majority language. As long as this sacred language maintains its importance, it will be effective in two distinct but complementary ways: it will still be taught and learned in the community; and it will continue to influence and interfere with the internal community use of the newly adopted language. This notion of a special status for the language of the sacred texts was well established among Jews, continuing to endorse the unsuitability of a Gentile language to deal with Jewish life until it had been modified and made Jewish.

The process has been analysed most fully in the case of Yiddish, in the magisterial study by Weinreich (1980), but it shows up in the development of other Jewish languages as well. Its clearest exemplification is in the use of words and phrases from Hebrew, or, at later stages, from the Hebrew Aramaic that is usefully labelled *lashon kodesh*, to refer in particular to specifically Jewish concepts or objects. The Aramaic spoken by Jews in Palestine and elsewhere was marked in this way, allowing for the easy switches between the two languages which can be seen in the Babylonian Talmud. There is good reason to suspect that Judaeo-Greek, the language that Jews of Italy came to speak, and the Judaeo-Romance that developed from it shared similar features.

Weinreich's analysis of Yiddish draws attention to the fact that it is most strikingly differentiated from the Middle German dialects from which it grew by its use of *lashon kodesh* to deal with what he calls 'the Way of the Shas', the specifically Jewish aspects of life. The most obvious examples of this are found in a number of pairs of terms where a word of Germanic origin is used to express a general concept in Yiddish, whereas a word of *lashon kodesh* origin is used for a Jewish version of that concept. Thus, any book is a *bukh*, but a Jewish book is a *sefer*; a teacher is a *lerer*, but a teacher of Jewish subjects is a *melamed*; bread is *broyt*, eaten on the ordinary weekdays (*Montik* or *Donershtik*), but on *Shabes* the Jew eats *khale*.

We note here an illustration of the principle, suggested to me by Carl Voegelin, that borrowing a foreign word for an alien object may in fact represent acculturation without assimilation. By building up a parallel set of lexical items, where the foreign word refers to the imported item, the native term is kept for the unchanged, traditional item. If this is correct, it draws attention to the fact that the linguistic purists who decry the borrowing of foreign words may actually be hastening the integration of alien concepts and objects, and so the loss of traditional culture.

One of the critical distinctive features of Jewish languages, then, has been their readiness to use *lashon kodesh* as a barrier against assimilation. A rather regrettable concomitant effect of this has been to emphasize the non-autonomy of Jewish varieties by highlighting their admixture of two valued languages, the standard varieties of *lashon kodesh* and of the co-territorial vernacular. At its least, this leads to the complex pull that Yiddish has suffered towards its two higher-status sources, Hebrew and German, and, at its worst, it accounts for the unwillingness to recognize the Jewish variety as a real language, the tendency to label it as a dialect form of the co-territorial vernacular, or as even less, a 'jargon'. The inevitable result of this has been the particularly low status and value attached to the Jewish variety, and, therefore, reduced language loyalty and maintenance.

Jewish languages permitted Jews to maintain their community identity, with a useful internal diglossic functional distribution between an H variety (*lashon kodesh*) and an L variety (the Jewish language), while learning and using co-territorial vernaculars and even co-territorial H varieties (Goyish) for external relations. Basically, this pattern seems to have been true of the Jewish communities throughout the Middle Ages. Hebrew or *lashon kodesh* maintained its special place as the internal language for H functions; co-territorial languages were learned as required or permitted; Jewish varieties served internal L functions. The challenge to the pattern came in the train of Jewish emancipation, starting in the middle of the eighteenth century with the lessening of external barriers to assimilation, and the Haskalah, or Enlightenment movement, which began in the 1700s and brought with it a threat to the strength of internal Jewish values. These social and intellectual pressures appeared linguistically in the pull towards standard European languages and associated values in nineteenth- and twentieth-century Germany and France and even more strongly in the English-speaking world.

The development of political meaning for language choice, the tie between language and nation and language and ethnic group which accompanied the rise of nineteenth-century nationalism, reached its acme in the ideological-political basis of language choice faced by Jews in pre-revolutionary Russia: the old three-language pattern, with internal Yiddish and *lashon kodesh* and an external co-territorial vernacular for those who remained committed to the old traditions; Russian for those who believed in universalism and revolution; a revitalized Hebrew for those who believed in socialism and Jewish national liberation in Eretz Israel; and Yiddish without *lashon kodesh* for those who believed in a new Jewish secular nationalism.

To summarize: we see that Jewish multilingualism clearly pre-dates the destruction of the Second Temple in 70 CE. By the first century a pattern had developed whereby Jews knew and used Hebrew for religious and literary purposes, spoke a Jewish vernacular, and also, as members of a minority group, knew and used non-Jewish languages. This pattern is true of Jerusalem in the second half of the nineteenth century.

3

The Socio-Linguistics of Old Jerusalem: Non-Jewish Languages in the Late Nineteenth Century

JERUSALEM within the walls, which we have chosen, albeit somewhat arbitrarily, to define as the area of our study, was in actual fact the major part of the city until the later years of the nineteenth century: the first houses were built outside the Old City only in the 1850s (see Ben-Arieh 1979: 93 ff.; Ben-Arieh's books are a major source of information on nineteenth-century Jerusalem, and my debt will be apparent). The walled city of today is closely connected in all ways to the city outside the walls: whether for work, or education, or as social or political limits, the gates of the city, closed nowadays only for traffic or other emergencies, serve to join the communities inside to those outside, rather than to divide them. But until the late nineteenth century this was not the case: the gates were shut every night (Ben-Arieh 1984: 21–3), and the walls defined the extent of the city.

Throughout its existence, the city of Jerusalem, though small and closed, has been rich in its linguistic complexity. In the time of the Second Temple, as Chapter 2 has shown, four languages (Hebrew, Aramaic, Greek, and Latin) played defined and distinct roles. During the period of the Crusader kingdoms the linguistic varieties served as the basis for social and political organization. Jerusalem in the twelfth century was a 'kaleidoscopic microcosm of contemporary Europe and the Near East'; while the French were predominant, there were many other linguistic groups—Spaniards, Provençals, Italians, Bretons, Germans, and Hungarians—each living in their own special quarter (Prawer 1972: 71). Under the Ottomans, too, a rich pattern of multilingualism developed which lasted, with some modification, into the twentieth century.

We learn of the pattern under the Ottomans from Jewish visitors who visited the city in the seventeenth century. In 1650 Moses Porges (Preger) wrote that Sephardim (in the narrow and more precise sense, Jews who trace their descent from the community expelled from Spain in 1492), who made up the larger part of the Jewish population, were the ones who ran stores, while the small group of Ashkenazim (Jews with a Central or East European background) did not know enough Arabic to trade with the other peoples. To do business, you needed to know 'Shpanyilish' (or 'Judezmo', the term preferred by scholars like David Bunis, Joshua Fishman, Tracy Harris, David Gold, and Max Weinreich for the language of the Sephardim, rather than the names 'Ladino' or 'Judaeo-Spanish' favoured by other scholars, or 'Spanyol' or other terms used by the speakers of the language), 'Rapish' (Arabic), and 'Tirkish' (Turkish). This same trilingual pattern is reported later in the century by Rabbi Gedalya Semyatitsher (cited by Kosover 1966, whose book is an excellent gateway to the study of the language history of Jerusalem in modern times), who lived in Jerusalem from 1699 until 1706: the Jews, he said, spoke Sephardic (Judezmo), the Arabs spoke Aramean (Arabic), and the Ishmaelites (Turks) spoke Ishmaelite (Turkish). He, too, went on to say that Ashkenazim did not trade because they could not speak these three languages, and the other inhabitants of the city did not speak Yiddish. The Moghrabim (North African Jews) who adapted their native North African Arabic to the local vernacular, and the Morisco Jews who had lived in Palestine for centuries and spoke the local variety of Arabic as their native language had a hard enough time making a living, but life was even worse for the Ashkenazim:

We are among them like the mute who is speechless and like one who does not understand their language. We are strangers, not admitted among Jews and more so among the nations. And when we buy some food from an Arab in the market, he gesticulates with the fingers. We answer in like manner by hinting to him, and they make a laughing-stock out of us . . . (Semyatitsher, quoted in Kosover 1966: 101.)

About 125 years later one finds the same pattern reported by another Jewish visitor: 'These three languages are there in use: first, the language of the Ishma'elites; second [the language of] Portugal, which is spoken by Jews called Frenken, and, third, Arabic. This language is spoken in all transactions by townspeople and city people alike.' (Translated from Kaminicer 1839.) James Finn, British Consul in Jerusalem, called attention to the linguistic richness of Jerusalem in the presidential address to the Jerusalem Literary Society on 23 December 1853: 'We have too in Jerusalem an unequalled field for languages. Venice and Constantinople might produce as great a diversity of tongues in the places of public resort, but certainly not the depth of tone and historical value attached to those of Jerusalem.' (Finn 1878, ii. 112.) He enumerates: 'Hebrew and Greek, Turkish and Arabic, Syriac, Abyssinian, Hindustani, Russian, German, French, Italian, Spanish and English (and other languages) are daily spoken in Jerusalem.' (Finn 1878, 2: 103.)

Similar wonder at the linguistic wealth of Jerusalem is listed among the 'principal difficulties encountered' by Charles Warren in his exploration of the archaeology of Jerusalem:

The languages spoken in Jerusalem are most confusing. The hotel-keeper talks Greek; his cook, Amharic; one waiter, Polish-Hebrew; another Italian; another, Arabic; the barber speaks French; the washerwoman, Spanish; the carpenter, German; the dragoman, English; and the Pacha, Turkish; Sepoys from India mutter English oaths. Next to Arabic, the most useful languages are German and Spanish. (Warren 1876: 83–4.)

The English oaths are later explained as referring to an incident when a group of Blacks swore in English at Warren's assistant, who was wearing a British army uniform; he discovered that they were sepoys who had deserted from the Indian army at the time of the Mutiny (Warren, 1876: 110).

The linguistic opulence of the city is further shown by the fact that in 1881 there were, as reported in Luncz (1882), nine major religious communities in Jerusalem, each with its own head and language. Listed alphabetically these were: the Armenians, the Copts, the Greeks, the Jews, the Latins, the Muslims, the Protestants, the Russians, and the Syrians. Further bases for foreign languages were established by the ten consulates: American, Austrian, English, French, German, Greek, Italian, Persian, Russian, and Spanish. For pilgrims there were hospices in the Armenian convent, the Casa Nuova, the Greek convent, and the Coptic khan; there was also an Austrian and a St John's hospice, two 'houses for strangers' in the Jewish quarter, and pilgrim houses for Jews from Austria, Holland, and Germany on Mount Zion. Luncz also gathered figures that he considered to be 'approximately correct' of pilgrims to Jerusalem in the year 1879–80; their countries of origin are contained in Table 3.1.

TABLE 3.1. *Pilgrims in Jerusalem 1879–80*

Armenians	1271
Greek convent	
East Europe and Turkey	955
Cyprus	497
Elsewhere	266
Casa Nuova	
The East	415
Europe	392
America	22
Others	51
German and Austrian hospices	244
Russians	1510
Syrians	93
Hotel Fein	
English	103
Germans	41
Americans	28
Others	35
Other hotels	400
Jews (mainly Sephardim from the Caucasus)	430

Source: Luncz (1882).

As far as the late Ottoman period is concerned, the principal languages and the pattern of their use in the city might be summarized as follows:

Spoken Arabic. The vernacular; the native language of all Muslim and Christian Arabs, of Armenians, and of some Jewish minority groups, the practical language of government, used by all residents (except the newly arrived Ashkenazic Jews) as a lingua franca.

Classical Arabic. A written language, not widely known; the language of Muslim prayer and teaching.

Turkish. Official language of government, mainly restricted to higher ranks of clerks and the military, but used by the Muslim upper class as a second language, perhaps much as French was used by the aristocracy in pre-revolutionary Russia.

Greek. Written, religious, and educational language of Greek Orthodox Christians.

Judezmo. Principal spoken language of Sephardic Jews.

Hebrew (*lashon kodesh*). Written and religious language of all Jews, and language of intergroup communication for them.

Yiddish. Spoken (and written) language of Ashkenazic Jews.

Latin. Religious (and written) language of Roman Catholics.

English and German. Languages of the Protestant Churches and their missions and schools.

French. Language of Western culture, and the status second language of Westernized Arabs and Turks; the most widely used European language in the early part of the century (Bartlett 1844: 217).

Armenian. Religious and written language of Armenian clergy.

Portuguese, Italian, Spanish. Languages of Roman Catholic clergymen and friars. Italian was also useful as a language of wider communication (Bartlett 1844: 217).

These languages will be discussed in some detail in the pages that follow. Other languages that are attested as being in use include:

Aramaic. The religious language of the Syrian Orthodox Church and of some Syrian families.

Coptic. The religious language of the Coptic clergy.

Giiz. The religious language of Ethiopian clergy, who themselves probably spoke *Amharic* or *Tigrinya*.

Russian. The spoken language of the clergy of the Russian Orthodox Church, the religious language of which was *Old Church Slavonic*, and of the Russian pilgrims. There was space for 1,000 Russian pilgrims in the hospices in the Russian compound (Ben-Arieh 1979: 108). Luncz (1882) says that there were increasing numbers of Russian pilgrims, over 80 per cent of them women, coming to Jerusalem in about 1880.

There were also a good number of other languages spoken by individuals and by the various Jewish immigrant groups arriving in the latter part of the century.

We have no language censuses, nor accurate census of any kind before 1916, but Table 3.2, based on Ben-Arieh (1984), contains estimated population figures for the nineteenth century. It should be noted that Jews came to make up half the population of Jerusalem within the walls by 1870, and the majority within and

TABLE 3.2. *Population of the Old City in the nineteenth century*

	1810	1835	1880	1900	1910
Muslim	4,000	4,500	7,500	10,500	12,000
Greek	—	1,600	3,300	5,000	5,900
Roman Catholic	800	900	1,750	2,850	3,560
Armenian	500	520	710	850	1,300
Coptic	50	—	100	130	150
Ethiopian	13	—	75	100	100
Syrian	11	—	15	70	100
Protestant	—	—	470	1,000	1,600
Sephardim	2,200	2,600	8,000	16,000	20,000
Ashkenazim	—	650	9,000*	19,000*	25,000*

* Jewish population outside the walls: 1880—2,000; 1900—16,000; 1910—29,000.

outside the walls after that. The Ashkenazic Jewish presence started to be significant after 1850. The Greek Catholic and Roman Catholic populations grew steadily during the period, with the main increase in Protestants taking place at the end of the century.

Spoken Arabic

Arabic remained the main language of the population even under Ottoman rule; only government clerks and members of the military forces were likely to know and use Turkish (Neumann 1877: 217–18, as cited in Ben-Arieh 1984: 186). Arabic was spoken by Christians and Jews as well as by Muslims. This was particularly true in the case of the Greek Orthodox Christians, who in the nineteenth century were local inhabitants who spoke Arabic and had Arab priests. Robinson (1841, iii. 453) reported that 'The language of the Greek Christians of Syria, both as spoken and as used in their churches, is Arabic. The spoken Arabic differs so little from the language of books, that all books written in a plain style, are intelligible to the common people.' But the services included technical terms in Greek, and some parts of the service were in Greek:

This is most frequently the case, when the high clergy officiate. It is an important fact, that nearly if not quite all the bishops of this sect are Greek by birth, and foreigners in the country . . . These bishops rarely learn to speak the Arabic language well; of course they cannot preach; and their medium of intercourse with the people in conversation is very imperfect.

Jews, too, knew Arabic. The Judezmo-speaking Sephardic Jews also knew Arabic, and the Moriscos were native-born Jews who spoke only local Arabic; they could recite prayers in Hebrew, but they did not understand them; and their knowledge of Arabic helped them to find employment. Jews born in Jerusalem, whether Sephardim or Ashkenazim, had the advantage not just of long-standing leases and earlier (and therefore higher) shares of the *halukkah* (charitable funds sent by Jews abroad to support their fellow-Jews in Palestine), but 'a thorough knowledge of the inhabitants, their language and customs, which makes commerce and all kinds of work easy for them' (Luncz 1882: 58).

The importance of Arabic as the lingua franca is clearly attested by the fact that lack of knowledge of Arabic was cited as one of the reasons for the continued poverty of the Ashkenazic Jews. In a letter written from Jerusalem between 1820 and 1824 Rabbi Israel ben Samuel from Shklov, a leader of the early Ashkenazic community, commented: 'As for us Ashkenazim, the Biblical saying "he hath made me dwell in dark places" was fulfilled. For we do not know the language, and we are all broken paupers.' (Cited by Kosover 1966: 103.) Wilson (1847, cited in Parfitt 1972) reported that no Ashkenazi living in Hebron, one of the four major Jewish communities in Palestine at the time of his visit in the early 1840s, could read or understand Arabic. But there were Ashkenazim living in Jerusalem who had grown up or lived in Safed, another of the major Jewish centres, who had learned some Arabic. A letter from Jerusalem in 1835 refers to sending Rabbi Shmuel, an Ashkenazi originally from Vilno who lived in Jerusalem, to escort a family from Sidon in Lebanon because he knew a little Arabic as a result of having lived in Safed as a child (Kosover 1966: 105). Wilson reports that while the Jews of Tiberias, the fourth of the centres, could speak Arabic, they could not write it.

To help ease the problems of new Ashkenazic Jews arriving in Jerusalem, the *Sefer Korot Ha'ittim*, published in Warsaw in a Yiddish edition in 1841 by Rabbi Menahem Mendl Kaminicer, included a short list of essential Arabic words: numbers, a few place-names, a few phrases, the names of some foods (Kosover 1966: 110). Newly arrived Ashkenazic Jews continued to have problems, however. A letter to Sir Moses Montefiore in 1874 pointed out that Ashkenazic Jews did not know Arabic and therefore could not engage in agriculture (Kosover, 1966: 113). But there were exceptions. According to the principal of the Laemel school (Ephraim Cohen-Reiss), the Ashkenazic *dayyan* (religious judge) Rabbi Raphael, who came from Safed, spoke excellent Arabic. As the century went on, Ashkenazic Jews who had come to Jerusalem while they were still young enough, or who had been born there, picked up spoken Arabic in the streets. In 1849 leaders of the Ashkenazic community sent a letter to Montefiore arguing against secular education and pointing out the uselessness of adding languages to the curriculum:

Do we not see with our own eyes, that it is impossible to make a living in this country from the knowledge of foreign languages? We have already with us quite a few of our own people who write and speak French, German, Polish and Russian thoroughly, and actually starve, and are compelled to receive charity from the community funds. As for the languages of this country (Arabic, Spanyolish), our children are thoroughly familiar with them indeed. There are also to be found businessmen who know them. (Baron 1937: 305, quoted by Kosover 1966: 111.)

The Sephardic Jews did, however, learn Arabic: according to some, the only difference between the Laemel school in its early days and a traditional *heder* (Jewish elementary school for boys) was that Laemel taught Arabic and a little arithmetic (Ben-Arieh 1984: 343). The Sephardic Talmud Torah attached to the Doresh Zion school had five class-rooms and ninety pupils; it taught religious subjects, Hebrew, Arabic, and arithmetic (Ben-Arieh 1984: 344). The settlement outside the walls, Mahaneh Israel, was built for settlers from North Africa on the initiative of Rabbi David ben Shimeon (DVSH), who, at the age of 28, led a small group of immigrants from Morocco in 1854. By 1872 the community numbered 1,000, and by 1881 there were 1,300 (Ben-Arieh 1979: 145). The arrival of these Jewish immigrants from Morocco and of others from Yemen added to the number of Jews who knew Arabic, although their dialects were quite different from the local ones.

As part of his general efforts to establish the Jews of Jerusalem on a sound and independent economic base, Sir Moses Montefiore tried hard to improve their educational level and to ensure that they learnt Arabic and European languages. Reporting on the visit of Sir Moses, the British Consul James Finn wrote to Lord Palmerston on 22 August 1849:

A more determined opposition, however, was made to the establishment of schools for teaching European languages, Geography, Arithmetic, &c. They denied their need of such things, especially the Gentile languages, which would only expose them to the seductive arguments of the Christian missionaries. . . . it was my painful lot to overhear and to hear repeated numerous jests and perversions of Scripture in Hebrew applied to Sir Moses' own European costume and infringements of Talmudism. (Hyamson 1939: 133–4.)

Montefiore continued his efforts and managed to convince some of the leading Ashkenazic rabbis of the value of this education. But the opposition continued, as Noel Temple Moore, a subsequent Consul in Jerusalem, explains in a letter to Sir A. H. Layard (British Minister, Constantinople) dated 11 June 1879:

Some months ago, a sum of money was received from England by the Revd Rabbi S. Salant, Chief Rabbi of the Ashkenazim or German and Polish Jewish Congregations, for the purpose of providing the means of teaching the Arabic language to Jewish boys. Rabbi Salant and other Rabbis approved of the scheme, and arrangements were made accordingly, a teacher engaged, and instruction commenced.

Soon afterwards, however, a violent opposition was manifested by a faction, numerically small, who ill-treated the Teacher . . . They procured a decree . . . declaring the teaching of foreign languages to be unlawful, which they induced a certain Rabbi Joshua Diskin, an aged and learned Rabbi . . . to sign . . . the lessons were discontinued.

Moore spoke to Salant, who told him

that he and a large majority of his fellow Rabbis were in favour of instructing Jewish boys in the Arabic and Turkish languages, and appreciated the advantages that would result to them.

. . . the opposition proceeds from a small minority of Rabbis, mostly of the set of Khassidim, or 'the Pious', which is characterized by intense fanaticism, and composed chiefly of Hungarian Jews. Their motive seems to be a fear that the study of foreign languages would lure away the Israelitish youths from the study of their own sacred literature (Hyamson 1939: 405).

The Sephardic Chief Rabbi of Jerusalem (Abraham Ashkenazy) was unable to overcome this opposition, and wrote to the Chief Rabbi of Constantinople on 20 August 1879 reminding him of the *herem* (ban) of 1870 and the *herem* of 1873 forbidding the teaching of Arabic in Jewish schools in Jerusalem. Supporters of the ban, he said, were mainly Austrian, Hungarian, and Warsaw Hasidim. He could not overcome their opposition; he suggested writing to rabbis in Hungary to ask them to support the idea of an Arabic school and to use financial pressure on the communities (Hyamson 1939: 408–9). The decree forbade 'all instruction in foreign languages and in all subjects not strictly Jewish (even in the language of the country)'; when it was issued, it was read from house to house 'in Hebrew and in the Judeo-German jargon, to enable women to understand it' (Luncz 1882: 191). It applied also to parents whose children received instruction in German in a private school. Even though the plan to teach Arabic in the Ashkenazic Talmud Torah was not implemented, the Hasidim broke away and established a Talmud Torah of the Hungarian community. This conservatism of a section of the Jerusalem Ashkenazim was strengthened, Luncz (1882: 48) points out, by the fact that many of them had come to Jerusalem to flee the 'spirit of progress in the direction of European education' which was starting to affect so many European Jewish communities.

In a letter to Sir W. A. White dated 4 December 1885 Moore included a report on education. Jewish education was 'very backward', he said, and was mainly religious in character; only a few schools taught the elements of French, Arabic, and arithmetic. There were also very few schools that were run 'on ordinary principles', exceptions being the Alliance Israélite school, which had 150 pupils and taught Hebrew, French, Arabic, and English; the German Jewish orphanage, which had 34 pupils and taught Hebrew, Arabic, and German; and the Evelina de Rothschild school for girls, which had 160 pupils and taught Hebrew, French, and needlework (Hyamson 1939: 428).

As time went on, more and more Ashkenazic Jews did start picking up Arabic. One who grew up in the 1870s wrote later: 'In addition, I know one more language: Arabic, which I spoke fluently while still a child. I acquired it without the slightest effort on my part. We spent part of our life in the street, we mingled with Arabs, dealt with them . . .' (Frumkin 1940: 18–19, cited by Kosover 1966:

114). By the latter part of the nineteenth century Ashkenazic contact with Arabic had been sufficient to bring about those striking influences on their spoken Yiddish described in Kosover's pioneering study. The pattern is described in the preface to the statutes of Yegi'a Kappayim, a society of Jewish craftsmen founded in Jerusalem in 1906:

The first immigrants who arrived here 90 years ago, the majority of whom came from Lithuania and Russia, found a desolate and empty country . . . In addition, they were kept back from coming into contact with the native population by their lack of understanding of the language of the country and by their ignorance of its customs. As a result, they were unable to make a start towards their self-maintenance through business and other occupations, and they were compelled to exclude themselves and be separated from the rest of the population.

But for various reasons, an immigration to Palestine began after a lapse of 25 years. Among the many who arrived here were business people and craftsmen, who began to carry on the trade in the country and to introduce fabrication (industry) as well . . . They quickly acquired the language of the country and acquainted themselves with its customs and manners. And because they were responsible for their livelihood, they learned about their neighbours, and availed themselves of their knowledge, in order to get along with them in business. (*Statuten-bukh un Ordnungen funm Algemeynem fereyn Yegi'a Kappayim* 1906: 1–3, translated and cited in Kosover 1966: 114–15.)

Classical Arabic

It is important to stress that, while spoken Arabic was the main language of the city, knowledge of classical Arabic was in fact quite limited among Muslims as well as Christians and Jews. Robinson (1841) estimates that no more than 3 per cent of the Arab population were literate, and says that the classical language was not well known. There was no Arabic printing-press in Palestine or even in the whole of Greater Syria until they were introduced later in the century by Christians. In 1868 the Hebrew newspaper *Ha-Levanon* (5/26, 11 Tamus 1868, p. 413, cited in Ben-Arieh 1984: 136) reported a plan to publish an Arabic periodical that all sheikhs and notables would be required to read, but this plan was not put into effect.

Arab education was limited to reading and Qur'ān. In 1846 there were seven traditional Muslim *maktab* (elementary) schools alongside mosques, and there were six *madrasas* (high schools) adjoining the Temple Mount and forming a single institution. The Qur'ān was taught in them all. In addition, there were three *madrasas* in the city (Tober 1853: 449, cited in Ben-Arieh 1984: 137). This is confirmed by C. W. Wilson (1866: 45) ten years later; and Neumann's study of the city (1877: 234–77) reports the existence of eight to ten main elementary schools, some smaller ones, some *madrasas*, and no school for girls. These Muslim schools had 341 pupils in the late 1870s (Hartmann 1910: 65–75).

In the second part of the century Christian Arabs played a key role in raising the educational level of the Old City, both through the schools they established, which usually taught Arabic alongside their specific religious or national language, and through the printing-presses introduced into the city by the Armenians, Latins, and Greek Orthodox and used also to print in Arabic (Ben-Arieh 1984: 138). A new Arabic printing-house in the Franciscan convent was reported by Ritter (1866: 205).

In 1904 an official government newspaper in Turkish and Arabic was finally issued for Jerusalem and the Galilee, called *Quds al-Sharif*. In 1910 two Arabic newspapers, *Ansaf* (started a year or so earlier) and *Iqdam*, were closed by the government. In 1911 there was an Arabic weekly, *Al-Nafir*, as well as the government paper (Ben-Arieh 1984: 136–7). Only a few Jews were literate in Arabic. Rabbi Joseph Schwarz (1845) helped Rabbi Abraham Tzoref 'by composing clear, well-written petitions' to the King of Egypt in 1836. But this literacy in Arabic was rare. Only one out of fifty North African Arabic-speaking Jews in Haifa were reported by Wilson to be able to write the language.

Turkish

While Turkish was the official language of the Ottoman government, its use and knowledge were quite limited. The Turkish language seems to have had no real standing in Jerusalem: the Ottoman pasha in 1867 was characterized as a 'bigoted Muslim without French polish' (Warren 1876: 297); later pashas knew French. European visitors in the middle of the century saw no evidence of influence of the language after 300 years of Turkish rule. Arabic was needed to deal with any inhabitant of the Holy Land, Muslim or not. The Governors of Gaza, Jerusalem, and Hebron needed a Turkish secretary to read the pasha's *firman*. Only the offices of the pashas used Turkish; elsewhere Ottoman government bureaux used Arabic (Assaf 1941). Brosnahan (1963) claims that in the Ottoman-ruled Middle East Arabic was the effective language of administration; there was little incentive to learn Turkish, because only Turks were admitted to the highest level of administration where its use was required.

None the less, Turkish appears to have been the major language of telegrams. Luncz (1882: 136) gathered, 'after inexpressible trouble', the figures for telegrams sent to and from Jerusalem for the year 1881 (March to March, as the Turkish Post and Telegraph Office followed the Gregorian calendar); unfortunately, as Table 3.3 shows, he does not distinguish clearly between Turkish and Arabic. Luncz informs his readers that telegraph officials generally know French, Turkish, and Arabic; telegrams sent in other languages 'are often quite incomprehensible by the time they arrive here'.

In 1888 the municipality decided to build a theatre outside the Old City where plays would be staged in Arabic, French, and Turkish (Ben-Arieh 1984: 124);

TABLE 3.3. *Telegrams to and from Jerusalem in 1881*

	No.
Telegrams sent from Jerusalem	
For the Turkish Empire (official dispatches, unpaid for)	4,425
Private telegrams in the Turkish language	1,100
Private telegrams in European languages	835
Telegrams received in Jerusalem	
In Turkish and Arabic (official telegrams, not paid for)	9,390
In Turkish and Arabic (private telegrams)	1,000

Source: Luncz (1882: 136).

and 1904, as we have seen, saw the establishment of *Quds al-Sharif*, an official government newspaper in Turkish and Arabic for Jerusalem and the Galilee. The city's first Turkish government school, founded in the 1890s, catered for pupils of all religions, offering Arabic, Turkish, French, and basic sciences (Luncz 1892: 222–3, cited in Ben-Arieh 1984: 138). In 1915 the Salahiyyah high school and college was established in Jerusalem, the first modern school to stress Islamic studies. It served also as a teachers' college, and classes were taught in Arabic and Turkish (Tibawi 1972: 104–5; Grunwald 1975: 164–5; both cited in Ben-Arieh 1984: 138).

Greek

The major Christian community in the Old City was the Greek Orthodox, whose members, as already noted, were mainly Arabic-speaking. In 1838 the Greek Orthodox schools taught only ancient and modern Greek. Greek clergymen did not know Arabic well, even though this was the language in which local Arab Christians prayed (Robinson 1841: iii. 453–4). A Greek school for boys was opened with American help in 1842; it was intended for Greek Orthodox students, but had a small department for Muslims also. The school used Western methods, and taught a wider range of subjects than the earlier schools had done (Tobler 1853: 441–3, cited in Ben-Arieh 1984: 224). Luncz (1887: 88–9, cited in Ben-Arieh 1984: 224) says that a Greek boys school was started in 1848. A Greek Orthodox girls school was opened in 1862 (Luncz 1887). The Greek Orthodox schools' curriculum included reading and writing in Arabic, prayers, and selections from the Bible. There was a seminary for local clerics of low rank which taught Greek, theology, the Church Fathers, history, and geography. Literacy levels rose in mid-century, but the standard of education was low (Basili 1918; Assaf 1941; both cited in Ben-Arieh 1984: 224). In 1853 the Greek

Orthodox boys school had ninety pupils, and the college in the monastery of the Cross had fifty (Finn 1878: ii. 102). Bartlett (1855: 190) reports that the Greek Orthodox school in the Valley of the Cross monastery, founded four years before, was now in full operation. There were four teachers and ninety students, and the subjects offered included classical Greek literature, German, and French. The Baedeker guide (1876: 275) records six teachers, sixty pupils, and the subjects taught as including Greek, Latin, French, Arabic, and Hebrew. A Greek printing-press was opened at the Greek convent in 1853 (Petermann 1860–1: i. 192–200, cited in Ben-Arieh 1984: 224). In the 1870s the Greek Orthodox girls school had two female teachers and sixty pupils; the boys school three masters and 120 pupils (Baedeker 1876: 162).

Latin

In the nineteenth century the Roman Catholics in the city both were considered to be Arabs and spoke Arabic (Ritter 1866: iv. 204). The twenty monks in the Franciscan monastery of St Saviour were native speakers of Portuguese, Italian, and Spanish; the father superior was usually Italian, the vicar and procurator Spanish (Ben-Arieh 1984: 198). Prayers and sermons after the annual ceremony of the Holy Fire were therefore in several languages (Ben-Arieh 1984: 218). In 1846 the Franciscans received a press with Arabic and Latin typefaces from Austria; the first page was set in January 1847 (Petrozzi 1971: 64–9, cited in Ben-Arieh 1984: 230).

The St Saviour monastery ran a school where a local resident taught boys to read and write Arabic, and a friar taught them enough Italian and Latin to understand the rituals (Seetzen 1854–9: ii. 12). In 1831 there were fifty-two pupils in the school (Taylor 1855: 332–45, cited in Ben-Arieh 1984: 231). Franciscans at this time were mostly uneducated Spanish and Italian friars who, in spite of their long residence, did not know Arabic and were therefore at a disadvantage in the conflict which developed between them and the new Latin patriarchate established in 1846 to co-ordinate Roman Catholic activities (Petermann 1860–1: i. 217–18, cited in Ben-Arieh 1984: 232). There were two Roman Catholic schools in the early 1850s, one for children and one for adults. There was also a Latin seminary, which moved outside the city to nearby Beit Jala after 1853 (Finn 1878: ii. 102). The Franciscan school in Jerusalem had 150 pupils: lower classes studied Arabic, geography, arithmetic, and religion; upper classes studied Italian, French, and literature. Most local Catholics knew Italian (Neumann 1877: 306–8, cited in Ben-Arieh 1984: 233). In 1884 Eliezer Ben-Yehuda served as a go-between when Rabbi Wittenberg wanted to buy two houses near the Damascus Gate from the Latin Patriarch, who knew only French (Ben-Arieh 1984: 379).

French

French was the language of Western culture: the Ottoman pashas after 1876 could speak it (Robinson 1841: i. 422); plays were performed in it in the theatre built in 1888 outside the Old City (Ben-Arieh 1984: 124); it was taught in the government school (Luncz 1892: 222–3, cited in Ben-Arieh 1984: 338); it was taught in higher classes in the Franciscan school (Neumann 1877: 306–8, cited in Ben-Arieh 1984: 233); it served also as a language of wider communication (Ben-Arieh 1984: 379). There were also French institutions: the Latin hospital was called the French hospital by Reicher in the 1860s (1870). Until the Berlin Congress in 1878, France and Britain had backed Turkey politically. The French Consulate, established in 1843, was the third to open its doors in Jerusalem: the first was the British (1838); the second was the Prussian German (1842). The church of St Anne was built in the 1860s on a site presented to the French Consul by the Sultan (Ben-Arieh 1984: 172). The Catholic procession at Easter included hymns in French (Ben-Arieh 1984: 218).

Armenian

The long-established but small Armenian community in the Old City took education seriously: they had a school for boys and girls as early as 1846 (Ben-Arieh 1984: 247). In 1866 there were eighty boys in the school who were studying Armenian and Arabic. In the nineteenth century Arabic was the colloquial language of the Armenians, and Armenian was only spoken by the educated. The Armenian printing-press was set up in 1833. It published in Turkish and Armenian (Ben-Arieh 1984: 248). The revival of spoken Armenian and, ironically, the introduction of spoken Turkish are results of the influx of Armenian refugees following the massacres by the Turks at the outbreak of the First World War (Azarya 1984).

English and German

The introduction of both English and German into the Old City was associated with the Protestant missions and Churches. The first Protestant Bishop of Jerusalem, a Prussian Jewish convert, was appointed in 1841. He was succeeded in 1846 by Bishop Samuel Gobat, a Swiss who spoke English, French, and German (Warren 1976: 100) and who served until 1879; this joint bishopric lasted until 1887, when it was dissolved and the Protestant Churches started to function independently (Ben-Arieh 1984: 251). The language issue was a source of considerable friction. In the late 1840s the early service on Good Friday was in

Hebrew, attended by twenty converts, with the remaining services being held in English and German (Strauss 1947: 171–80, cited in Ben-Arieh 1984: 261). In 1851 a German traveller complained about what he saw as an Anglican take-over of Protestant activities, and the increasing use of English; he claimed that in the Protestant mission school German-speaking Polish Jewish converts were learning English and forgetting German (Ben-Arieh 1984: 252). Morning prayers in Christ Church, for which the attendance was higher, were in English, whereas the afternoon prayers were in German. There were about 200 Protestants in Jerusalem in 1853. There was a Hebrew service every morning at 6.00 a.m.; English and German services on Sunday; and plans for an Arabic service. To attract Judezmo-speaking Jews, there was also, in 1853, a Sunday service in Spanish (Bartlett 1844: 47–8, cited in Ben-Arieh 1984: 262).

When Warren visited Jerusalem while pursuing his archaeological explorations, services in Hebrew, Spanish, English, and German continued, but the Arabic service had not yet come about. He saw English as being in danger because the mission now employed only Germans: 'Look at the results of this system: the Germans have increased and multiplied, until, at the present day, at Jerusalem, they number three hundred, while the English are quite out of the field.' (Warren 1876: 94.)

English

Bishop Gobat built two schools, one for fifteen girls and one for forty boys. The teachers were English, Arab, and German (Stewart 1857: 301–4). They taught English, geography, and Scripture to the boys, and sewing and other subjects to the girls (Ben-Arieh 1984: 257). The Baedeker guide (1876: 231–2) reports that the pupils included Arab orphans. Orelli (1878) reports that the school was run by the Bishop's wife. The language of instruction was English (Ben-Arieh 1979: 95). There was also an attempt to establish an English college in 1854; the pupils (Jews, Syrians, a Maronite, a Greek deacon, Jewish Christians) had no real common language, so German, Italian, and Arabic were all used, but by the end of the first term English alone was sufficient. The college was closed after a year, when its headmaster returned to England (Finn 1878: ii. 105–8).

German

Quite apart from the fact that German was used by the Protestant Church, the language was also widespread in the Holy Land and Jerusalem because many Jews spoke German.

The latter part of the century saw the establishment of more German institutions. Orelli (1978: 191–4) reports that there were seventy boys between the ages of 4 and 17 in the Schneller orphanage, where the languages of instruction were Arabic and German (Ben-Arieh 1979: 104). The use of

German in Jerusalem was increased by the establishment of the German colony by a group of German Templers in the latter part of the century. The first Templers, a dissenting Protestant sect from the south of Germany, arrived in Palestine in 1860, and a group established a residential area in Jerusalem in 1878. There were about 300 of them living in the German colony in the last decades of the century, working in various trades and professions (Ben-Arieh 1979: 178–83). Another German foundation built outside the walls was Talita Kumi, a girls school. With the separation of the German and English Protestant missions, this became an important institution, with a curriculum based on those in Germany. Its girls learned Arabic and German, and their parents or guardians signed guarantees that, once admitted, the pupils would continue in the school until they had completed their studies. In 1876 there were between seventy and a hundred girls in the school; the girls were reported to wear European clothes (Orelli 1878, cited in Ben-Arieh 1979: 185). By the outbreak of the First World War there were 141 girls in the school, the vast majority (128) of whom were Arabs, but including five Armenians and four Syrians. Only fifty-one were Protestant; eighty-eight were Greek Orthodox (Ilan 1972, cited by Ben-Arieh 1979: 185). There were also a number of German hospitals and shelters. A German Evangelical school was started in the Russian compound in 1873 with eleven pupils, and taught a regular German elementary curriculum: there were forty-one pupils by 1879 (Ben-Arieh 1979: 189).

In describing the socio-linguistic situation of the Old City towards the end of the nineteenth century, we have concentrated so far on the major non-Jewish languages, whether spoken by Jews or Gentiles. By 1880, however, Jerusalem had a Jewish majority, so it is appropriate to consider the use of the major Jewish languages in a separate chapter.

4

The Socio-Linguistics of Old Jerusalem: Jewish Languages in the Late Nineteenth Century

THIS chapter will look in particular at the status of the three major Jewish languages spoken in Jerusalem in the nineteenth century. As background, we will first sketch the make-up of the Jewish population of the city in 1881, choosing that year to take advantage of the detailed description provided by Luncz (1882) in his first year-book, originally prepared to answer a set of questions posed by the Board of Deputies of British Jews in 1876.

Leaving aside the Karaites, a small Jewish sect which rejected Talmudic Judaism, Luncz divided the Jewish population into Sephardim and Ashkenazim: the former were subdivided into Sephardim proper, who spoke Judaeo-Spanish, and Moghrabim, who spoke Arabic; the latter differed from the Sephardim, he said, by ritual and by the fact that they spoke Judaeo-German. It is interesting to note that he found this language division to be the major distinguishing characteristic of the communities. According to Luncz, there were 7,620 Sephardim, of whom 1,290 were Moghrabim, having come from the Maghreb or North Africa. As a rule, they were natives of the city, Turkish subjects, and fluent in Arabic. Apart from the *chachamim* (a total of 290 families, including eighty-five Moghrabim), the heads of whose households were exclusively engaged in Jewish sacred study, all Sephardim were self-supporting. The *chachamim* shared in the general *halukkah* according to their personal status and learning, and also received a share of the *halukkah* of the *yeshivah* to which they belonged. The class as a whole was generally prosperous—some were even rich, while the poorer also received payment for devotional duties and were 'above actual want'.

The second major classification of the Sephardim, according to Luncz, was the tradespeople, who tended to be engaged in commerce or labouring rather than handicrafts. In 1877 there were 242 families in trade (58 drapers, 49 grocers, 24 money-changers, 18 fancy-trimming makers, 15 pedlars, 13 cookshop-keepers, 10 clerks, 7 fowl- and egg-dealers, 5 each in vegetables, wine, and old furniture, 4 each in tobacco and second-hand clothes, 3 booksellers, to mention the main groupings), most of whom lived comfortably, with few of them poor. Another 200 families were in crafts, including 27 tailors, 21 tinmen, 15 shoe-makers, 33 cobblers (some itinerant, most Moghrabim), 9 goldsmiths, 10 nurses, 7 law-court practitioners, and 12 servants in private houses. This group also lived above the poverty level. Unskilled labourers comprised a third group of 92 families among the gainfully employed, 51 of whom worked as porters and 23 as bakers' assistants. The final group was made up of those who worked for the community, receiving also a share of the *halukkah*. This group accounted for 98 heads of families, including 30 teachers, 17 meat-salesmen, 4 writers of *tefillim* (phylacteries) and *mezuzot* (religious scrolls), 17 'writers for the communities and for private people', and 20 communal beadles and servants.

The third social division among the Sephardim was made up of the 'widows, orphans, infirm persons and the respectable poor', some 125 Sephardic households and 100 Moghrabim, all receiving assistance from the community. Some worked, others were recognized beggars. In a fascinating aside, Luncz calculated that a beggar needed to visit 480 houses to obtain enough for a day's requirements. Finally, Luncz mentioned two small Sephardic subdivisions, the Georgians and the Jews from Aleppo, each with their own language and synagogue.

Luncz estimated that by 1880 there were 6,660 Ashkenazim in Jerusalem, forming a community that had essentially come into existence in seventy years, and the bulk of which had arrived in the last twenty-five. The majority came from Russia and Poland, and most of the rest from the Austro-Hungarian Empire; only a small minority had come from Germany and Holland. The Ashkenazim were divided into two main classes, the Talmudic scholars and the aged, and the tradespeople. Most of the first group, he said, was made up of 'the aged, who weary of this life's troubles, have given up all business and have come to Jerusalem to die here in peace and to be buried on the Mount of Olives in view of the site of our holy temple' (Luncz 1882: 49). Some brought money with them, or had interest sent from money invested at home; others depended entirely on the *halukkah* and on irregular remittances from home. Some 255 families received income from communal offices, including 13 *dayyanim*, 27 paid presidents, 15 *shochetim* (ritual slaughterers), 60 teachers, 24 writers, 35 *batlanim* (scholars paid to study in memory of the dead), 63 *yeshivah* students, and 18 beadles.

Merchants constituted one section of the Ashkenazic tradespeople: 215 families in all, most of whom were engaged in buying and selling locally, including 47 grocers, 21 wine- and spirit-dealers, 10 tobacconists, 20 flour-dealers, 23 bakers, 16 milkmen, 10 butchers, 10 brokers, 12 mill-owners, 7 corn-dealers, 5 money-changers—two of whom Luncz ranked as bankers—9 trimming-dealers, and 4 booksellers. A second group was made up of handicraftsmen; 364 workmen, with generally high standards, including 46 tailors, 45 shoemakers, 42 joiners, 35 turners, 22 writers of *tefillim*, 14 goldsmiths, 12 compositors, 11 tinmen, 11 watchmakers, 10 printers, 8 barbers, and so on. Luncz pointed out that, in fact, there were too many craftsmen to meet the community's needs: many found it difficult to make enough money to keep their families. The third group were the labourers: 215 families who made up the poorest class, including 37 day-labourers, 18 labourers in mills, 6 porters, 25 regular beggars, and 120 'odd-jobmen or idlers'.

Judezmo

Spanyolish or Judezmo was the first and main language of the Sephardic Jews; Gentiles were reported to understand it, and many Ashkenazic Jews learned it. There were prejudices against it, however, as a 'corrupt Spanish patois' (Baedeker 1876: 89). A letter from Jerusalem in 1834 advised that those planning to come (from Germany) should learn some Italian ('which is related to the Spanyoli language of the majority of the Sepharadim here . . . and . . . understood by the Gentiles as well': Kosover 1966: 101–5). The first British Consul reported in 1839 that Jews used Spanish and Arabic; contracts and other writing were in Hebrew (Kosover 1966: 111). The fifteen Karaites living in a single courtyard on Rehov Ha-Yehudim in the 1820s were reported to be able to speak Judezmo. When a Jewish vocational school was set up in the early 1850s, it had separate classes for Sephardim and Ashkenazim, each group of which studied in the spoken language of its community. Rabbi Isaac Ezekiel Yehuda, giving testimony before the Wailing Wall commission in 1929, recalled memories from fifty years before. He said, among other things, that 'Poor Sephardi scholars would sit there all day long and read to people in . . . Ladino. The old men and women sat around in a circle to listen.' (Ben-Arieh 1984: 312.)

As a result of the arrival of Oriental and Ashkenazic Jews, Judezmo, initially the native language of the vast majority of the 2,000 Jewish inhabitants, declined in relative use in the course of the nineteenth century until it represented the mother tongue of only a third of the Jewish population of the Old City (Ben-Arieh 1984: 356–7).

Hebrew

Both the extent and the degree of knowledge of Hebrew before the revival, or, more precisely, the revitalization, at the end of the nineteenth century (see Chapter 5) are often underestimated. Montefiore's diary gives some idea of the standard of Hebrew outside Palestine. In 1828 he visited a school in his native Leghorn, reporting that 'Most of the seniors, although not yet fourteen, are perfect masters of the Hebrew language and can write in the same on any subject of their studies that may be given them.' (Loewe 1890: 54.) Even in England there were those who understood Hebrew. In June 1828 a 'messenger' from 'a theological college in the Holy City', the 'Rev. A. J.', visiting London to collect money, was invited 'to deliver a discourse in the Portuguese synagogue . . . [He] gave an interesting discourse to the community in pure Biblical Hebrew' (Loewe 1890: 57–8).

Reports from the British consular representatives attest to the importance of Hebrew as a language of wider communication in Jerusalem in the nineteenth century. The first British Vice-Consul, William T. Young, appointed in September 1838, arrived in Jerusalem in March 1839, and soon made clear the need for a Hebrew dragoman in a letter he wrote to the British Foreign Secretary, Viscount Palmerston, at the end of May: 'The languages in which the Jews chiefly communicate are Spanish and Hebrew—contracts among them and their writing generally are done in Hebrew.' (Hyamson 1939: 7.) The request was disputed by Colonel Campbell, the Consul-General in Cairo, who argued 'that not only is Arabic the language spoken, and in use in all documents between the generality of Jews in Palestine, but even the greatest number of Jews there are ignorant of Hebrew and which language is never made use of, written or verbally, in the common relations of life'. Young responded vigorously to this in July:

I would most respectfully observe that this is not in accordance with my experience. As for instance this week was brought before me two documents in Hebrew. One was the will of a deceased pereson, the other was a statement of property . . . In the case of the Jewish community versus Rabbi Mizrachi . . . the chief of the documents were in Hebrew, and I have now before me a case where, though the document be in Arabic (because it is between a Christian and a Jew) the Jew signs in Hebrew. I might quote other instances and may refer to the mode of conducting Jewish affairs among themselves which I believe, for so I am informed, is entirely in Hebrew, and which ancient custom they are very tenacious of and desirous to maintain. (Hyamson 1939: 16.)

Palmerston subsequently approved Young's request, authorizing the appointment of a Hebrew dragoman in the Vice-Consulate at an annual salary of £30 (Hyamson 1939: 24), though by the time the approval came, Young had already paid out £10 from his own pocket for interpreting (ibid. 27). The work of the interpreter is detailed in later letters; for instance, in 1840, when Young reported in a letter to Palmerston that he had had the Loyal Address and the Queen's reply translated into Hebrew for the Jewish community and enclosed a reply from the community with a translation (Hyamson 1939: 30).

But problems with interpreters continued. Though fluent in Hebrew himself, Young's successor, James Finn, found it necessary in 1849 to use several Hebrew translators rather than one: 'In the exercise of my discretion I have not paid 30 pounds sterling a year to one Hebrew Dragoman but have used part of that sum to remunerate other Hebrew translators in cases where on account of factions unhappily so rife among the Jews it would not be safe to employ any one person for every business . . .' (Hyamson 1939: 127–8). Finn had learned Hebrew before he came to Palestine; he continued to study it throughout his period of office as Consul, and attended the Hebrew services in Christ Church. He also claimed to be able to read Judaeo-Polish and Sephardic dialects and scripts, and knew Arabic and Turkish: 'It was no small satisfaction to me that not only Hebrew, but the extraordinary medley of languages called *Juedisch*, both oral and written, was intelligible to my own family without an interpreter . . . This was an advantage to be found in no other Consulate.'

Writing in the middle of the century, he attested to the vitality of Hebrew:

With regard to pure Hebrew, the learned world in Europe is greatly mistaken in designating this a dead language. In Jerusalem it is the living tongue of everyday utility— necessarily so, for in what else could Jewish strangers from opposite ends of the earth converse to each other? In our Consular office, Hebrew was often heard spoken—on one occasion by a Jew from Cabool [Kabul], who had to enter into explanations with one from California: of course in Hebrew. That language was a medium of transacting business in the English Consulate. (Finn 1878: 127–8.)

On a visit to Tiberias, the Ashkenazic and Sephardic Elders spoke about the visit of Sir Moses Montefiore to the site of the Temple in Jerusalem:

On this topic they spoke to each other with eyes sparkling, and only in Hebrew; no other language seemed to satisfy the glow within their minds—the run of the sentences I understood so as to put in a few words with them occasionally—but with us they mostly spoke in Arabic or German (not choosing to use the Holy Tongue with Gentiles). (Finn 1878: 360.)

A good knowledge of Hebrew was a major advantage, especially when being called upon to represent the community abroad in fund-raising: 'a Sephardi Chacham as Messenger from Jerusalem is much more esteemed than an "Ashkenazi" of the same standing as the former speaks our holy language with much more facility and address [*sic*] which gives him a wonderful advantage, especially among the Jews of the West' (Luncz 1882: 37). The usefulness of Hebrew is further confirmed by the fact that, on a number of occasions, the English missions aroused the ire of the local Jewish community by posting placards in that language. On 19 December 1871 the British Ambassador in Constantinople wrote to Noel Temple Moore (the Consul in Jerusalem) about the 'affair of the Hebrew Placards' (Hyamson 1939: 368). Further, a letter from Moore to the Secretary of State for Foreign Affairs, dated 19 October 1876, reported that 'The Placards in question are printed in Hebrew; as explained to me by [Revd] Mr Frankel [in charge of the English mission] they contain statement of a controversial character seeking to prove to the Jews from the Old Testament that they are in error . . .' (Hyamson 1939: 400). Moore asked Frankel not to post them, and the Earl of Derby, the Foreign Secretary, approved this action (Hyamson 1939: 402).

While Hebrew was known and used by the Jews, differences in handwriting and pronunciation were sufficiently marked to cause problems. In 1848 James Finn reported in a letter to the acting British Consul-General in Syria that 'The former [Sephardim] despise the latter [Ashkenazim], and disdain to learn their vernacular dialect or to write their alphabetical character. My official Dragoman, though a Rabbi and the eldest son of the third Rabbi in Jerusalem, is unable to read or write even the superscription of a letter in the Ashkenaz character.' (Hyamson 1939: 127–8.) In 1850 the British Consulate forwarded a petition from the Moghrabim saying that they needed their own synagogue because both their form of prayer and Hebrew dialect were different from those of the Sephardim (Hyamson 1939: 163). A similar argument was cited by James Finn when transmitting a request from the Ashkenazim to rebuild the Hurvah synagogue: 'These numerous people, above 2000 souls, have not even one synagogue in Jerusalem, for although the Sephardim Jews (being mostly Orientals and Turkish Subjects) have Synagogues, they have their ritual books and their pronunciation of Hebrew different from these . . .' (Finn 1879: 225–6).

Yiddish

The Ashkenazim who started to move into Jerusalem in increasing numbers in the nineteenth century brought with them many languages, but on the whole they used Yiddish, a language sometimes seen by non-Jews as 'German with the peculiar Jewish accent' (Baedeker 1876: 89). Ashkenazic Jews spoke the same language as they used abroad, and followed the same dress and manners. As we have already mentioned, not knowing Arabic and Judezmo was a handicap that lasted until family life was well established in Jerusalem.

As time went on, the pattern of daily life for a well-integrated family was responsible for adding other languages to Yiddish. Here is a description of the language pattern of an Ashkenazic Jewish family in Jerusalem in the 1870s:

Yiddish was the spoken language of our house. The occasion to speak Hebrew, or as it was called, Loshn Koydesh, was seldom at hand. It was used only when there was need to interrupt one's prayers . . . or when one had to carry on a conversation with a Sephardi, not knowing his language, Spanyolish. At any rate, everyone in our house, both great and small, spoke a fluent and idiomatic Yiddish . . . Another language, which was almost the second spoken by us, was used in our family: Ladino, or Spanyolish. This happened because we had in our house a domestic servant, a Sephardi woman . . . and also because my father's sister . . . was married to a Sephardi and all her family spoke only Spanyolish . . . I know one more language: Arabic, which I spoke fluently while still a child. I acquired it without the slightest effort on my part. We spent part of our life in the street, we mingled with Arabs, dealt with them . . . (Frumkin 1940: 18–19, translated and cited in Kosover 1966: 114.)

Yiddish eventually came to play a significant role in the life of the Old City, and was widely known: 'The 250 tiny crowded stores on the Street of the Jews were owned largely by Ashkenazim who could freely use the language they had spoken in the Diaspora. Even the Sepharadi Jews and gentiles who had business on this street spoke Yiddish.' (Yellin 1972: i 15–16, cited by Ben-Arieh 1984: 385.) As noted above, the British Consul James Finn was also proud of his knowledge of Yiddish (Finn 1878: 127).

Continuity and discontinuity

The Old City of Jerusalem in the nineteenth century was multilingual. The main spoken language was Arabic, but Judezmo, Yiddish, and, in some cases, Hebrew also served as languages of wider communication. The government's use of Turkish was minimal, but it was constrained to use Arabic and other communal languages as well. Each religion pursued its activities in a formal religious language, but, alongside that, it often made use of a national European language: the Christian Churches were a principal source of literacy in European languages and in Arabic as well. At the beginning of the period the Jewish community was mainly trilingual: Judezmo as the spoken language, Hebrew for religious purposes and for literacy, and Arabic for outside activities; early Ashkenazim maintained the Yiddish–*lashon kodesh* diglossia, the traditional functional separation that they had brought with them from Europe, and were slow to add a new co-territorial vernacular as the third member of the set. As time went on, the Ashkenazim too learned Arabic, and Yiddish became a trade language for non-Ashkenazic Jews and for Gentiles. Hebrew had a respected role as a language of communication across Jewish communal boundaries, but the development of modern spoken Hebrew is a phenomenon that occurred outside the walls.

If we compare this picture of the Old City in the latter part of the nineteenth century with our description in Chapter 1 of the same area a hundred years later, some major discontinuities become apparent. Nineteenth-century Jerusalem was contained essentially inside the walls; in 1980 the city between the walls was only a small part of a larger metropolis. In 1880 most of the population of Jerusalem lived within the walls—17,000 of the 30,000 crowded into this space were Jews; in 1980 Jews made up only 13 per cent of the 27,000 people living in the Old City, but Jerusalem as a whole had a population of 400,000, 80 per cent of whom were Jewish. There are also major discontinuities of population to be noted. The Jewish population of the Old City in 1980 includes very few of those who were living within the walls before the Jordanian conquest of 1948, although there are a number of children of people who had lived in the Old City. At least a third of the Muslim population over the age of 50 was also born elsewhere, as were half of the Arab Christians over the age of 50. Given the density of population and the general crowding, those who could afford it tended to move out of the Old City into the newer suburbs. There was no development of the Old City's infrastructure during the Jordanian period (the paving of the streets and the replacement of the water and sewage systems took place in the 1980s), and people continued to move out or to be replaced by immigrants.

One major continuity lies in the unbroken dominance of Arabic as the spoken language of the majority within the walls. There have been major changes, however. First, there has been a large increase in Arabic literacy. Second, the fact that Hebrew is the dominant language of the surrounding area means that Arabic speakers tend to know Hebrew as a second language. Third, English has triumphed over the other European languages as the most useful second language.

Within the Jewish community the greatest discontinuity has been the establishment of Hebrew as the principal language of daily life. This development, building on the basis outlined earlier in this chapter, occurred—paradoxically—not in Jerusalem, where it might have served as a useful lingua franca between Ashkenazim and Sephardim, but in the ideologically strong Zionist settlements like Petah Tikva and Rishon Le-Zion, where Yiddish speakers made a conscious effort to shift to the new, revitalized language.

For the minor languages the changes have been different. The Turkish massacres of Armenians in the early part of this century had two effects: the influx of a number of secular Armenians, so that Armenian became a spoken language, and, ironically, the influx of native speakers of Turkish. The other minority languages face serious challenges from Arabic (among Muslims and Christians) or Hebrew (among Jews).

The main continuity is that the Old City is still, one hundred years later, a basically multilingual society: the status and make-up of the multilingualism has changed, but the fact of its existence continues.

5

The Revitalization and Spread of Hebrew

ALTHOUGH the ravages of the Roman–Judaean wars had substantially depleted the Jewish population of Palestine, and although many of those who remained were converted to Christianity during the Byzantine period, a remnant of Jews survived and continued to live in Palestine until modern times. Their numbers were augmented at various times over the centuries by Jews from Diaspora communities returning to Palestine either as a possible place of asylum from persecution or in order to pray, study, or to be buried in their ancestral home, a wish to which their daily prayers made reference. Until the nineteenth century, however, immigration was small and sporadic, and poor local conditions—economic, health, and security—under the various foreign rulers meant that remigration was probably substantial (Bachi 1977: 77).

Increased external pressure and a slight improvement in local conditions led to continuous Jewish emigration in the nineteenth century, with perhaps 25,000 Jews arriving between 1850 and 1880. This represented a sizeable increase in the small total population of Palestine, estimated to have reached 532,000 (of whom 43,000 were Jews) by 1890 (Bachi 1977: 32, 77). This Jewish population was divided, as we have noted, into several communities, each with its own language pattern. Jews from Eastern Europe spoke Yiddish; Jews from the Ottoman Empire and the Balkans spoke Judezmo (Ladino); Jews from Africa and Asia spoke their own local varieties of Arabic. But all of them shared, as we have discussed earlier, a knowledge and use of Hebrew.

Although Hebrew was no longer a language in daily spoken use, it had retained its place in most Jewish communities as a language to be read and to be written, to be prayed in, and to be studied. While it was the pre-eminent language for religion, it was used in secular domains as well: in the composition of legal, scientific, and philosophical texts, and, with the development of the Enlightenment, for secular *belles-lettres*. An immense number of books were in fact written in Hebrew throughout this period, and the language continued to develop and change to meet new demands. It is interesting to note that the first Hebrew novelists in the nineteenth century set themselves the enormously demanding task of writing in the limited Hebrew of the Bible (Patterson 1989); later in the century, when they relaxed this limitation and accepted that modern Hebrew prose could draw freely on its linguistic evolution, the flowering of modern Hebrew literature began.

While it is true that, during the period when it was not a daily spoken language, Hebrew was restricted in its domains, serving mainly liturgical, scholarly, and literary functions, it was called on occasionally as a lingua franca by Jews who shared no other language: it served this purpose most especially in contacts between European Yiddish-speaking Jews and their fellows living under Muslim suzerainty. In nineteenth-century Jerusalem it seems to have performed this function in formal (and possibly informal) contacts between the established Ladino and Arabic-speaking Sephardic community and the newly arrived Yiddish-speaking Ashkenazim. There is some evidence of the development of Hebrew as a lingua franca among the Sephardim (Rabin 1973: 70), as some of the examples in the last chapter demonstrate.

Given this continued, if restricted, use, it is probably misleading, as Blanc (1968), Rabin (1973), and Fellman (1973, 1974) have pointed out, to refer to later events as language *revival*; *revitalization* might be a better term. Hebrew is no exception to the general rule that once a language has passed out of all use whatever, it remains dead. The 'revival' of Hebrew was its revitalization, the restoration of the vitality involved in being a mother tongue, its resuscitation as a vernacular, as the language of daily life, and especially as the language that parents speak to their babies.

The movement for the revival of Hebrew began in Eastern Europe and in Palestine in the latter part of the nineteenth century, influenced by European national movements, which viewed the language of a people as inseparable from its nationhood. There was, however, as Rabin (1973: 69) noted, an essential difference between the Hebrew revival movement and the language movements associated with European nationalism. In the latter cases, the usual task faced by the language revival campaign was to find a way to add literacy (H) functions and formal status to a spoken (L) variety of a language. In the case of Hebrew, the goal was reversed: to add spoken (L) functions to a language whose literacy status was already clear. Whereas the peoples mobilized by the European national movements could often be united by a common vernacular, the Jews were divided by theirs—but they could be united by appeals to the symbolic association of Hebrew with tradition and peoplehood.

A series of pogroms and repressive measures in Russia following the assassination of Tsar Alexander II in 1881 started a wave of mass emigration of Jews; some two million or so left Eastern Europe. Most found their way to America, but a small number came to Palestine, then a somewhat neglected outpost of the Ottoman Empire. Among them were young intellectuals, influenced by European nationalism and imbued with the notion of building a life in Palestine that was better than, and different from, the one they had known in Eastern Europe. It was these young Zionists who brought with them to Palestine the notion of using Hebrew as their national language, an all-purpose vernacular that would serve to mark the distinction from life in the Diaspora. The idea was first promulgated by Eliezer Ben-Yehuda, a young Russian Jew who arrived in the Promised Land in 1881. He was an indefatigable promoter of the revival of Hebrew, in his prolific writing, in his speaking, and in his own practice: he was the first to insist on using Hebrew at home and to raise his own children speaking the language. Ben-Yehuda himself lived in Jerusalem, but, with a few distinguished exceptions, his arguments fell on deaf or even inimical ears, as the bulk of the religious Jews in Jerusalem continued to favour the restriction of Hebrew to its sacred functions. It was to be in the new Zionist settlements that the revitalization of Hebrew was to take place.

The revitalization process

In a recent discussion of Hebrew language revitalization, Nahir (1988) proposes that there were four steps (or components, for they overlap) in what he calls the 'Great Leap' to Hebrew. First, the children of the community were 'instilled' with the required linguistic attitudes; second, they were presented (in school) with a model of language use; third, they themselves came to speak and use Hebrew, not just in school but also outside it, as a second language; fourth, when these children grew up, they started using Hebrew as the language of communication with their own children, who then grew up as native speakers.

Nahir documents each of these steps. The language choice in the new settlements, he claims, was essentially between Yiddish, the common language of the settlers, and Hebrew. Yiddish, however, was seen as a reminder of rejected features of Diaspora life, as vulgar, a jargon to be used and written only if you were illiterate in Hebrew. Hebrew was the language of the new nationalist movement, the language with a respectable literature, the language that expressed the national spirit. It evoked strong ideological support, therefore, especially among those settlers who had chosen to come to Palestine for nationalist reasons.

Nahir's notion of attitudes is clearly an important one. Ideology provides one major rationale underlying motivation, and it is worth trying to reconstruct the ideological situation at the time. The main conceptual dispute between Hebrew and Yiddish, which, Pilowsky (1985) says, was brought to Palestine from Europe, came to its full expression only at the beginning of the twentieth century, when it was fought out most bitterly within the labour movement. In 1907 Po'ale Zion (a part of the Labour party) issued two numbers of a periodical in Yiddish; this was strongly criticized by another faction, Ha-Po'el ha-Za'ir. The Labour party decided, at the end of a long debate in the summer of 1907, to issue its official journal only in Hebrew. It is significant that this decision was made one year before the Czernowitz conference, which Fishman (1980) holds as marking the establishment of an ideological basis for the Yiddish language movement; he dates the proclamation of Yiddish as an expression and symbol of Jewish national identity to 1902–5 (1980: 66). Fishman also points out (1980: 69) that it was possible to argue at Czernowitz that because Zionists who favoured Hebrew had not rejected Yiddish, the conference in its turn should not reject Hebrew; this was why the conference declared Yiddish to be *a* and not *the* national Jewish language. Thus, the vital decision about language choice had been made in

Palestine before Yiddish was ready, as it were, to enter the conflict ideologically.

It is important at this point to make clear the fundamental difference in the tasks undertaken by the proponents of Yiddish and Hebrew revival. For Yiddish, as with so many other European languages associated with national movements, the aim was to add, or approve the addition of, high-status functions to a widely spoken but low-status language; for Hebrew, the task was to add, or approve the addition of, daily use and speech (a low-status function which could be raised ideologically) to a language with high status. The dispute betwen the two sides was marked by strong rhetoric, and worse. In 1914, for instance, Chaim Zhitlowsky visited Palestine, lecturing in Haifa, Jerusalem, and Jaffa in Yiddish. The last of his planned series of lectures was disrupted by a demonstration of Herzliyyah high school pupils. In an article in *Ha-Ahdut*, Zhitlowsky argued that only Yiddish could maintain the unity of the Jewish people. In a reply, A. Hashin argued that Yiddish was not revolutionary; only Hebrew could be the national language. After the end of the First World War, supporters of Hebrew, concerned that new immigration from Europe would strengthen Yiddish, led a renewed ideological campaign. A proposal by N. Twerski that knowledge of Hebrew should be a prerequisite for election to the autonomous Jewish institutions in Eretz Israel was adopted at the Third Constituent Assembly of the *yishuv* (the Jewish community in Palestine) in December 1918. A meeting in Philadelphia of American Po'ale Zion, held at the same time, passed a resolution calling for equal rights for Yiddish in Palestine. The language question became a major issue in the struggle to unite the labour movement. It remained a central polemical issue until at least 1925. From 1925 until 1930 the debate in Palestine was much more personal, and attempts to found a chair of Yiddish at the Hebrew University in 1927 were defeated. The distinguished Hebrew poet, Nahman Bialik, who himself continued to speak Yiddish at home with his wife, was involved in the 1930s in a public incident with members of the self-styled Legion of Defenders of the Language.

The argument in Palestine was a continuation of a European debate, but the important decision was made by the labour movement before the Czernowitz conference. Extremists on each side held a monistic position, ignoring the possibility of multilingualism. It was essentially a struggle within the Zionist movement; the language question was not relevant in the conflict with the non-Zionists, who continued to use Yiddish. Ideologically, the Hebraists refused to allow any cultural role for Yiddish in Palestine, and the debates in the 1930s were intensely political. Later, in the 1940s, there was even violence, with a Yiddish printing-press being blown up. Paradoxically, after 1948, Oriental Jews came to identify the very élite which had chosen Hebrew with the Yiddish that they had rejected, seeing the latter as a symbol of discrimination.

These later ideological disputes give some idea of the nature and extent of the support for Hebrew in the period with which we are concerned, the kinds of attitudes that the Zionist settlers brought with them from Europe and passed on to the children in the Hebrew-medium schools, and the degree of motivation to learn and use the language that developed.

The second of Nahir's steps or components consisted of presenting the children with a model of Hebrew speaking, which followed from the decision to teach Hebrew in Hebrew, making use of the direct method. Until Eliezer Ben-Yehuda's brief spell as a Hebrew teacher in Jerusalem in 1883, traditional European Jewish teaching had always adopted the familiar practice of teaching Hebrew (and the Aramaic of the Talmud) through Yiddish, the pupils' native language. However, as Fellman (1973: 49) reports, Ben-Yehuda had worked for a few months in an Alliance Israélite Universelle school, using (at the suggestion of the principal, Nissim Bechar) the Berlitz (or direct) method of learning Hebrew through Hebrew. In the schools of the agricultural settlements, under the patronage of the Baron de Rothschild, the regular medium of instruction for general subjects after 1884 had been French, with Yiddish being used as the language for teaching Jewish subjects. There was no objection, however, when, in 1886, David Yudelevic emulated Ben-Yehuda and started teaching Hebrew in Hebrew. Texts were prepared; all general subjects were taught in his school in Hebrew by 1888, and by 1891 some subjects were being taught in Hebrew in several other colonies as well. In 1892 a meeting of the nineteen members of the Hebrew teachers' association decided that children of 6 should attend school for five years, that the direct method ('Hebrew in Hebrew') should be used, and that 'the explanation of the Bible is to be in Hebrew and in general all studies are to be explained in Hebrew' (Fellman 1973).

The next major step in providing children with opportunities to learn Hebrew was the opening of kindergartens or preparatory programmes. In 1892 the Baron de Rothschild opened a French kindergarten in Zikhron Ya'akov. Two years later, in 1894, a preparatory (pre-school) programme in Hebrew for 4- and 5-year-olds was instituted in Rishon Le-Zion. The teachers were untrained; their work is reported to have been unimaginative. In 1896 3-year-olds were admitted. A graduate of the school was sent to Jerusalem to be trained (at the Evelina de Rothschild school, in English); she returned in 1898 to open the first modern Hebrew kindergarten at Rishon Le-Zion, with thirty pupils. More Hebrew kindergartens were opened in Jerusalem (1903), Safed, Jaffa, Haifa, Tiberias, Rehovot, Zikhron Ya'akov, and Nes Ziyyonah (1904). Kindergartens became the main instrument for developing Hebrew fluency: 'Hebrew became almost the daily language of the youngsters' (Azaryahu 1910, cited by Fellman 1973); 'The child became the teacher of his parents, his brothers, his sisters . . .' (Chaim Zuta, cited by Fellman 1973).

A meeting of the Hebrew teachers' association in 1895 adopted Hebrew as the language of instruction, using Sephardic pronunciation (but Ashkenazic pronunciation was to be allowed in the first year in Ashkenazic schools, and for prayer and ritual). The next meeting of the association was not until 1903, at the close of a major convention of Jews of the *yishuv* called in Zikhron Ya'akov by Ussishkin, the Russian Zionist leader. The fifty-nine members present accepted Hebrew as the medium of instruction, and the direct method as the technique of instruction without much debate; there was general agreement also on the use of Ashkenazic script and Sephardic pronunciation.

So far, we have traced how Hebrew came to be used as a medium of instruction, but there is a second important issue to consider: what sort of model of Hebrew could, and did, these original Hebrew-medium teachers provide? In the early years there were no Hebrew teachers' seminars; the all-Hebrew teachers' seminar in Jerusalem was only established in 1904. How much Hebrew, then, could these early teachers have known? A recent proposal by Glinert (1987) suggests an answer to this question.

Glinert takes issue with the general 'Zionist-Hebraist' view represented by scholars such as Tur-Sinai and Avineri who have claimed that, before its revival, the Hebrew language was incapable of dealing with everyday life and who attribute this enrichment to the work of secular scholars and committees in the early years of the twentieth century. Glinert argues, rather, that there was in fact a semi-vernacular religious Hebrew already available and in use. The form and resources of this variety can be judged from Ganzfried's *Kitzur Shulhan Arukh*, an abridged and popularized guide to Jewish religious practice, first published in Hebrew in Hungary in 1864, of which more than twelve editions—400,000–500,000 copies—had appeared by 1908, including plagiarized ones. The *Kitzur* was taught in the traditional Jewish elementary schools in Europe and in Palestine, and covered the daily life of a Jew, all aspects of which were fully governed by religious law. It required Hebrew words for such everyday items as fruit, vegetables, and trees (some of which Avineri claims as later discoveries of the dictionary compilers) as well as other normal objects of daily life. Because the first Hebrew teachers in the settlements had themselves had a religious education, they would have known these words. Fellman (1973: 51) refers to the account of one of these early teachers, Izhak Epstein, who claims to have had little Hebrew education beyond elementary school; this education, however, included the Talmud until he entered high school, after which he read 'very little' modern Hebrew literature. Glinert (1987: 52) argues for the importance of this knowledge:

The very ease with which the Spoken Revival took place, and the will to do it, suggest the existence of a fairly nonliterary underlying model, not the highly complex and daunting system of Biblical Hebrew; add to this the less-than-scholarly nature of the teaching cadre, more at home with the unselfconscious 'unartificial' Hebrew of *Kitzur* and Rashi than with grammatical treatises or Enlightenment fiction . . .

We suspect that not just the teachers but also the parents of the children in the first Hebrew classes were likely to have had a similar educational background, and so to have been familiar with the 'semi-vernacular' that Glinert postulates; this would obviously be a major factor in providing the children with a wider model and in establishing the possibility of their later use of Hebrew at home. It is also intriguing to note, as Weinreich (1980: 311) does, that while the revitalization of Hebrew involved a separation from the Diaspora and from the Yiddish that represented the Diaspora, it was mainly Yiddish speakers who were the pioneers of modern Hebrew; building on the complex pattern of functional allocation that existed between Yiddish and *lashon kodesh* (Fishman 1976), they were able to draw on both languages as they started to use Hebrew as a daily language. It would be ironic and fitting if continued research were to establish that the contemporary Hebrew language owes its basic Indo-European bent to the Yiddish with which it successfully competed for loyalty.

The third step in Nahir's model was the stage at which the children in the Hebrew-medium classes took Hebrew outside the school: first, they started speaking Hebrew not just with their teachers but also with each other outside school, and then with their parents and other adults. This involves overcoming what Spolsky (1989: 162) called 'the inertia condition' on language choice, a strong preference to continue using the same language to the same person. Once the children started to speak freely in Hebrew in the class-room, this condition would favour speaking it to each other outside. It would, however, require considerable effort to overcome the inertia of home-language practice, and we will return to this.

Nahir (1988) provides documentation on the stages of language-spread outside the school. Progress was slow at first; Smilansky (1930) reports that in 1891 Hebrew-school graduates stopped speaking Hebrew when they left school. But ten years or so later the situation had changed. Azaryahu (1910) claims that Hebrew had become the 'children's tongue', though not the children's mother tongue. Haviv (1910) reports that Hebrew was spoken in the streets and homes of Rishon Le-Zion. Hazikhroni (1902) reports that in Zikhron Ya'akov young men and women also used Hebrew. Feinsod-Sokenick (1929) says that the kindergarten children brought Hebrew into the home; the mothers then took evening classes in Hebrew. Pirhi (1905) reports on a 2-year-old who spoke only Hebrew and sang songs in it; she was teaching her parents all she knew. By 1912, Klausner (1915) claims, all young men and women could read a Hebrew newspaper. As time went on, a number of language islands appear to have developed; by 1902 Zikhron Ya'akov was a place where Hebrew as a second language was the language at least of the young, but as late as 1907 a newspaper article there expressed surprise that public speech was given in Hebrew, considered to be the normal language of children in the settlement but not of adults.

The next step was the crowning one, as graduates of the Hebrew-medium schools, for whom Hebrew had become the regular second language (and the main first language with each other), married and started to communicate with their children in Hebrew. This change must have happened between 1905 and 1915. Bachi (1956) says that 40 per cent of Jews (34,000 of 85,000) recorded Hebrew as their first or only language in the 1916 census; the figures are higher

(75 per cent) among the young. As we define it, then, the process of language revitalization took between twenty and twenty-five years, and while there remained a great deal to do to develop Hebrew as a full, modern, spoken and written language, the basis had been well established. Both Nahir's thesis and the research data that we have sketched provide a plausible hypothesis about the nature of this successful revitalization. It also points the way to much-needed research into the internal situation in the settlements, the birthplace of the process: were they in fact monolingual in Yiddish, or was there an obvious need for Hebrew as a lingua franca? Can we establish the educational and religious background (in Europe or Palestine) of the parents of the first generation of Hebrew-speaking pupils? We have some studies showing how the language spread from the settlements, how first the Hilfsverein and later the Alliance schools admitted Hebrew, culminating in the language riots over instruction in the Haifa Technion (see below, p. 72), but studies of the early years would help to confirm the general picture that has been painted here, or show how it must be modified.

Reasons for the initial adoption of Hebrew

Cooper (1989), in his comparison of the Irish and Hebrew cases, stresses the material incentives for the adoption of Hebrew, that is, the inherent value of Hebrew as a lingua franca in the growing Jewish population of the *yishuv*. Similarly, Fishman (1980: 55) downplays the importance of ideology:

Intellectuals (and even an intelligentsia) alone can rarely establish a movement. Intellectuals can reify language and react to it as a powerful symbol, as the bearer and actualizer of cultural values, behaviors, traditions, goals. However for an L to spread into H functions more concrete considerations (jobs, funds, influence, status, control, power) are involved.

If this could be established in the case of Hebrew revitalization, it would simplify our task, but the evidence does not fully support it. Rather, the socio-linguistic situation in those settlements where Hebrew was first taken outside the class-room seems to suggest that this most critical of all steps took place in communities where Yiddish was already a satisfactory language of communication, where no lingua franca was needed, for it occurred not in the mixed Ashkenazic/Sephardic towns like Jerusalem and Tiberias, but in the mainly Yiddish-speaking agricultural settlements.

As we have already said, detailed studies of these communities in the key years may clarify this point. In the meantime, however, other possible explanations must at least be canvassed. First, it is vital to stress (following Rabin 1973) the difference, referred to earlier, between language revival as a general phenomenon and language revitalization. The task in the Hebrew case was to take a language with virtually no vernacular use and no native learning, but a language generally known in its written and learned forms, and add the spoken function; in other words, to add L functions to an H function. With Irish and Maori, however, we are dealing with a language with decreasing vernacular use and dying native learning, but no widespread knowledge of the classical or written version. This may be compared to the analogous, but more complex, task undertaken by those who set out to add high-culture functions to the Yiddish used in everyday life (Fishman 1980); it must be recalled that the arguments at Czernowitz were not that Yiddish should be a spoken language (it was), but that it should be used as a vehicle for high culture. With Irish, this was to lead to increased knowledge, but not to a reversal of the decline of the spoken language; in a sense, the effect of the Irish language movement (and, one suspects, of many other modern language restoration movements) has been to provide the necessary institutions to bring the language to a situation not unlike the one from which Hebrew language revitalization started.

A second critical issue to note is the nature of the competing language. Both Irish and Maori were unfortunate enough to be competing with English, one of those languages that in the twentieth century (and particularly in the latter half of it) has shown its power to spread universally, offering itself as an attractive alternative (or at least, necessary complement) to most other languages in the world. During the period of Hebrew revitalization the opposing languages were less powerful. Yiddish was the language that Hebrew replaced as a vernacular, but it was in many ways, as we have suggested earlier, a pre-ideological Yiddish, a Yiddish plainly (to the people concerned) labelled as not just a language associated with the Diaspora (the denial of which was their very reason for being in Palestine), but a language lacking (at least before 1905) clearly acknowledged cultural value; indeed, many hardly considered it a language at all, but a jargon. The religious culture that used Yiddish as a vernacular valued Hebrew more highly, although Yiddish was recognized as having a limited but important status in educational functions (Fishman 1980); the secular culture that used Yiddish for daily speech valued non-Jewish languages like French and German more highly. Nor were there strong arguments for Judezmo (which turned out to have quite a low language loyalty) or Arabic (for Jews in most Muslim countries had been restricted to vernacular and low-valued varieties). In other words, Yiddish, Judezmo, and Arabic were all perceived as L varieties in competition with one or more H varieties, while Hebrew already had the status of an H variety. In the Jewish schools of the *yishuv* there were two serious competitors for secular teaching, French and German. The strength of French was sapped by the withdrawal of the Baron de Rothschild in 1899; some opposition to his control was expressed as early as 1887, in arguments for the use of Hebrew in Rishon Le-Zion. The strength of German dated from the inauguration of the Hilfsverein schools in 1901; even from the beginning, however, there was strong ideological support for Hebrew here, especially in schools outside the city (Fellman 1973). And it was in these schools that the language war, the struggle over whether to use

Hebrew or German as the language for higher scientific instruction, was fought in 1913–14.

A third critical factor was the extent and breadth of the teachers' knowledge of Hebrew (in its H functions). The language they knew was not the Hebrew of the intelligentsia, the H variety of Enlightenment literature, but a combination of religious varieties, ranging from the high formality of the Bible to the semi-vernacular of the religious commentaries and codes of practice in which so many of them had been educated. Their task in starting to speak Hebrew with their pupils was not dissimilar (but in many ways easier) from that of the formally trained foreign-language scholar on a first visit abroad—not an easy task but, given the strength of motivation, an achievable one.

Finally, therefore, we suspect that it was not so much material conditions as the strength of motivation, arising from stronger ideological commitment, that accounts for the initial success of Hebrew language revitalization. Successful revitalization would seem to depend on establishing a sufficiently high solidarity value for the language being revived to overcome any power or economic effects of the competing language. There is reason to believe that the ideological arguments for Hebrew were strong enough to overcome not just the ideological arguments for French and German (and, later, for Yiddish), but also any perceived power or economic values of all the competing languages; ultimately, it was sufficiently powerful to overcome some of the inertia condition and to make parents ready to switch to their children's language.

The spread of Hebrew

Between 1881 and 1903 some 20,000 to 30,000 Jews arrived in Palestine (Bachi 1977: 79). As we have seen, Ben-Yehuda's idea of using Hebrew as the language of instruction was adopted in the new settlements that they founded. By 1910 the first graduates of these schools, who were fluent and natural in Hebrew, had begun to marry each other; the first generation of children who spoke nothing but Hebrew in the home was being born: 'They were the first people, after a lapse of 1,700 years, who know no language but Hebrew.' (Rabin 1973: 73.)

During the First World War immigration to Palestine came to a virtual halt, but it started again after 1918, when Palestine was occupied by Allied Forces and was removed from Turkish rule. The League of Nations awarded the mandate to control Palestine to the British government in 1922; the British divided the territory into two, proclaiming the eastern sector as a separate kingdom of Transjordan, where they set up Abdullah as king. The territory west of the Jordan River, in the former Turkish *sanjaks* of Acre, Nablus (Shechem), and Jordan, was established as Palestine. The British Mandate government proclaimed English, Arabic, and Hebrew to be the official languages of Palestine.

During the period of British occupation the population of Palestine doubled, from about 670,000 in 1919 to 1,970,000 in 1947 (Bachi 1977: 40). Both Jews and Muslims, the two major sections of the population, showed the same absolute increase—600,000 each—but in relative terms this was a much greater increase for the Jewish population, which grew in size elevenfold, from about 56,000 in 1919 to about 650,000 in 1948 (Bachi, 1977: 40). This high rate of increase among Jews was mainly due to immigration. During this period most of the immigrants came from Eastern and Central Europe, initially for political and economic reasons, but after 1933 because of Nazi persecution. British government policy in 1939 set limits to this immigration, limits which continued in effect even as the outcome of the Holocaust became public after 1945. There was also a substantial Jewish immigration from the Yemen and other Asian countries at this time.

In 1948 the British government gave up its mandate, and a United Nations decision led to the partition of Palestine and the establishment of the state of Israel. The second element of the United Nations decision, assuming the creation of an independent Arab state, was not carried out; rather, part (Gaza) was occupied by Egypt, and the remainder, including the Old City itself, was occupied by Transjordan (later renamed Jordan).

The first act of the newly established state of Israel in May 1948 was to repeal the British restrictions on immigration, and an enormous wave of settlers followed. Survivors of the Holocaust, unwilling or unable to remain in Europe, were now able to enter the new Jewish state. At the same time, a growing sense of insecurity among the Jews living under Arab rule in Asia and North Africa, bolstered in many cases by Messianic expectations, led to a mass exodus. During the first three and a half years of the existence of the state of Israel close to 700,000 Jews flocked there, more than doubling the population (Bachi 1977: 79); and the rest of the 1950s through to the end of 1960 saw the arrival of another 300,000 (ibid.). Altogether, from independence in 1948 until the end of 1978, more than 1,600,000 Jews came to Israel, about two and a half times the number of Jewish inhabitants before independence. In 1950 immigrants constituted approximately 75 per cent of the Jewish population in Israel; by 1978 this figure had declined to about 45 per cent.

Cooper's (1984) discussion of the spread of Hebrew consists of the succinct question: who adopts what, when, where, how, and why? Let us consider each of these in turn. The study of the demographic characteristics of those adopting Hebrew permits a number of generalizations. Among immigrants, the younger they were when they arrived and the longer they have been in Israel, the more likely they are to use the language now. For immigrants who arrived during the British Mandate period, those who came from Arabic-speaking countries and from Eastern Europe were most likely to use Hebrew; those who came from Austria, Germany, Hungary, and Turkey were less likely to use Hebrew. Among those who arrived after 1948, the index of Hebrew speaking remained high among Jews from Arabic-speaking countries, but the index for persons from

Eastern Europe declined. Schmelz and Bachi (1974) suggest that this decline can be explained by the collapse of organized Jewish education in Eastern Europe under Nazi and Soviet rule, and the fact that earlier immigrants tended to have had a Zionist ideology. The high indices among immigrants from Arabic-speaking countries are explained in part by the relationship between Arabic and Hebrew, two Semitic languages, an affinity which helps a speaker of one learn the other vernacular. The lower indices among immigrants from Austria, Germany, and Hungary can be explained in some measure by the strong cultural ties with German and Hungarian on the part of those Jews whose communities had been assimilated for a long time (Bachi 1956: 230–1), as well as by the greater ability of German speakers to use their mother tongue or cognate English to earn a living (Hofman and Fisherman 1971).

Younger people are more likely to use Hebrew than older people, both because they are more likely to have been born in Israel and because they have a higher level of formal education. Formal education appears to contribute to use of Hebrew in a number of ways—many well-educated immigrants had studied Hebrew abroad and in formal situations in Israel—but it is neither a necessary nor a sufficient condition, as witnessed by the many highly educated German-speaking immigrants who resisted the adoption of Hebrew, and the many poorly educated or illiterate immigrants from North Africa and Asia who adopted it with alacrity. Perhaps the main reason for the link between education and use of Hebrew can be found in the fact that those occupations involving a working knowledge of Hebrew are also those for which a formal education is required. Thus, managerial and clerical workers and people in the liberal professions, especially teaching, show comparatively high indices of Hebrew use, while workers in the service occupations, such as traders, salesmen, tailors, shoemakers, and unskilled workers, show low indices (Schmelz and Bachi 1974: 778–9).[1] The influence of occupation on the use of Hebrew can be seen from the 1961 census. Among Jews aged 14 and above, the index of Hebrew speaking was higher among those with employment than for those without employment, for those who worked at least thirty-five hours per week than for those who worked less, and for those who worked for more weeks in the year than for those who worked fewer (Schmelz and Bachi 1974: 778).

There is good evidence to support the contribution of linguistic heterogeneity to the spread of Hebrew, just as Brosnahan (1963) showed its relevance as one of the four conditions promoting the spread of Greek, Latin, and Arabic in the empires associated with those languages. The influence of linguistic heterogeneity can be seen in a survey carried out among 190 adults in eighty Romanian-speaking Jewish families from three communities in Israel (Hofman and Fisherman 1971). About half of the families had been in the country for more than twenty

---

[1] We will note in a later chapter a striking contrast with Palestinians' knowledge of Hebrew; in the Old City study we found that it was those in the service occupations who had the better control of Hebrew.

years, and the other half for three to six years. Among the newcomers, those who lived in Jerusalem, where they were scattered all over the city, knew more Hebrew than those who lived in the town of Nahariyyah, where they were concentrated more homogeneously. Among the earlier immigrants, those who lived in Nahariyyah, the home of many ethnic groups, knew more Hebrew than those who lived in a nearby rural settlement populated mainly by Romanian speakers.

Linguistic heterogeneity has long been a feature of the Jewish community in Palestine and Israel. Taking account of the principal languages claimed by respondents in the 1916–18 censuses, Bachi (1956: 197) estimated that if any two Jews met at random during that period, the chance that they would share the same principal language was only about one in three. Hebrew was already (Bachi 1956: 194) the most common principal language by then (40 per cent), followed by Yiddish (36 per cent), Arabic (18 per cent), and Judezmo (4 per cent). There is a good chance that Hebrew was also the chief lingua franca among the Jews of Palestine by that time, for it was the language most likely to be shared by interlocutors who did not have any other language in common.

When the state of Israel was established in 1948, the probability that two speakers drawn at random from the Jewish population would share the same principal language had increased from 32 per cent (at the close of the Ottoman period) to 58 per cent (Bachi 1956: 177). Hebrew was by then the principal language of the bulk of the Jewish population. But while the linguistic homogeneity of the Jewish population as a whole was increasing, the trend was in the opposite direction with the non-Hebrew-speaking immigrants. The linguistic heterogeneity of the immigrants became more marked during the British Mandate and especially during the period of mass immigration after independence, partly because of the larger number of languages spoken by immigrants, and partly because of the marked erosion of Yiddish. Whereas the censuses of 1916–18 had confirmed that nearly 60 per cent of all Jews who did not speak Hebrew as a principal language spoke Yiddish, by 1972 that figure had dropped to 19 per cent for those aged 14 and above (Bachi 1977: 290). Of the eight languages listed by Bachi (1977: 290), Yiddish is the only one whose percentage of use among non-Hebrew speakers has declined in each of the five periods studied between 1916 and 1972—even between 1948 and 1954, when large numbers of Yiddish-speaking immigrants arrived.

Perhaps the rapid decline of Yiddish has stemmed in part from its low status (see above, pp. 59–61) and in part from its decreasing usefulness as a lingua franca. As Greenberg (1966) has pointed out, the more people who use a lingua franca, the more useful it becomes and the more it exerts pressure on others to learn it too. Conversely, nothing stops the spread of a lingua franca more surely than the existence of a rival. The growth of Hebrew as a lingua franca at the end of the Ottoman period, then, would have created pressures for its acquisition and slowed the spread of its chief rivals, Yiddish and Arabic. The potential of Yiddish as a lingua franca was almost certainly undermined, in addition, by its association with the ultra orthodox anti-Zionists of East European origin, who used it as their internal lingua franca.

Modern Hebrew shows relatively little differentiation among speakers when it comes to everyday, informal conversation, and, at the same time, relatively great differentiation between formal and informal varieties. Unlike Palestinian Arabic, which varies from town to town and from village to village, there is virtually no geographic variation in modern Israeli Hebrew, save for a few shibboleths like the Jerusalem pronunciation of the word for 'two hundred' and names of some children's games. Two major varieties of Hebrew are generally recognized: general Israeli Hebrew and Oriental or Sephardic Hebrew, the latter identified by a few pronunciation variants which are stereotyped markers of membership in Asian and African ethnic communities. More and more Jews from these communities are now adopting the general pronunciation (Bentolila 1983; Blanc 1968), but the differences are very slight when compared to regional and social dialects in England, for instance. The relative lack of differentiation in informal Hebrew speech, whatever its cause, has simplified the learning process and contributed to the speed with which the vernacular has spread.

If the homogeneity of informal spoken Hebrew has simplified learning, the substantial difference between spoken and written Hebrew and between informal and formal varieties has complicated the task of mastering the latter varieties. The distance between the two is much greater than in English, but not so great as between the informal and formal varieties of Arabic. While knowledge of the informal language can be picked up by interactions in the everyday world of market-place and work-place, knowledge of the more formal varieties depends essentially on education. This is particularly related to the status of Hebrew as a revitalized language. As Rabin (1975) has pointed out, Hebrew's status as a literary language is ancient and continuous, whereas the vernacular tradition is discontinuous, having suffered an interruption of 1,700 years. During this long period literacy in Hebrew meant literacy in a classical language. Vernacular literacy is something new. The Hebrew grammar which Israeli children study in school, for example, is not the grammar of the modern vernacular, but a normalized systematization of biblical Hebrew carried out in the thirteenth century (Rabin 1983). It is noteworthy that the two best descriptions of the modern language have been published in English rather than in Hebrew. Formal Hebrew varieties, the immediate heirs of this ancient literary tradition, exhibit substantial differences from everyday Hebrew in vocabulary and grammar. Thus, the radio news is presented in a variety of Hebrew somewhat remote from that used in everyday speech: the language of the newspaper is also quite different from everyday speech.

Among immigrants, then, it is not surprising to find that the Hebrew of everyday speech is learned more easily than the Hebrew of newspapers and radio, and language-usage data gathered by Rosenbaum (1983) support this. Similarly, the study by Hofman and Fisherman (1971) found much more knowledge of spoken Hebrew than of written; length of residence in Israel accounted for an increase in spoken ability, but not in written, which was dependent on formal education instead. The differences between informal and formal varieties probably represent a more serious problem among immigrants arriving after about 1930. Before then, most male immigrants were likely to have had a formal religious education and so to know literary Hebrew. Those who came later were less well prepared.

From the beginning, Hebrew seems to have spread from public to private domains. In 1902, twenty years after Ben-Yehuda arrived in Palestine, there were only ten families in Jerusalem who spoke Hebrew at home (Rabin 1973: 70). Jerusalem, of course, as we have already noted, was much more conservative in this respect than the new Jewish settlements. Still, it is evident that the first use of Hebrew was in a public setting, the schools. It is likely that the language entered the home only when the graduates of these schools married each other. Among immigrant families, there is similar evidence that Hebrew enters the home through the children who learn it in the street and at school; when they come home, they continue to use it among themselves and with their friends, and finally insist on using it with their parents. A mother of three, for example, who arrived from Germany as a young woman in the 1930s and whose children were born in Israel, reports that she spoke German to her first child, who answered in German; she spoke German to her second child, who answered in Hebrew; and she spoke Hebrew to her third child.

Hebrew is now the dominant language in public settings. A survey of language use on a street in West Jerusalem (outside the walls) (Rosenbaum *et al.* 1977) noted that about half of those heard speaking Hebrew did so with a marked non-native accent. Public language use on that street could be predicted by the following rule: speak Hebrew unless your mother tongue is English and you are speaking to another mother-tongue speaker of English (a language which enjoys special status in Israel; see Cooper and Fishman 1977). Although most shopkeepers knew English, most native speakers of English switched to Hebrew to carry out their transactions. Between Jewish Israelis who do not share the same mother tongue, Hebrew is the virtually unchallenged lingua franca.

Efforts to promote Hebrew

Considerable efforts are made to help new immigrants to Israel learn Hebrew: the government subsidizes Hebrew courses, and a substantial proportion of immigrants enrol; special classes are offered to new immigrant children. In addition, some of the news broadcasts are transmitted in simplified Hebrew spoken at a slower rate than normal, and there is a weekly newspaper in simplified Hebrew.

Whereas these efforts to promote the spread of Hebrew are now mainly concerned with helping immigrants to learn the language, organized language-spread activities were of a different character in the early part of the century. There were at least three types of activity. First, there was a move to modernize the language and to standardize new terms. This work, started just a hundred years ago by the Hebrew Language Council, continues today in the work of the formally constituted Academy of Hebrew Language. Second, there were the efforts of teachers and pupils in Jewish schools to establish Hebrew as the language of instruction; this culminated in the 'language war' of 1913, which Rabin (1973: 75) characterized as the 'first national struggle' of modern Jewish Palestine. A German Jewish foundation for the advancement of Jews in technologically underdeveloped countries, the Hilfsverein der deutschen Juden, was developing plans to establish a technical high school in Haifa. The foundation already operated a number of schools in Palestine, in all of which Hebrew was used as a language of instruction. None the less, in planning the curriculum of its new tertiary technical institute, the foundation felt constrained to promote German as a language of culture; it announced in 1913 that the new *Technikum* would use German and not Hebrew as the medium of instruction, on the grounds that Hebrew was not sufficiently advanced for work in the sciences. This gave rise to strong resentment, expressed particularly by teachers and students in other Hilfsverein schools, who proclaimed a boycott. The foundation was forced to reconsider its plan and to accept that Hebrew should be the medium of the new curriculum.

The third type of organized effort involved encouraging people to use Hebrew. For instance, a youth organization called the Gedud meginnei ha-safah (Legion of Defenders of the Language) was founded in 1923 to combat the use of languages other than Hebrew; it remained in existence until the late 1930s (Wigoder 1972: 1000).

At least until the victory of Hebrew in the language war, and probably well into the period of the Mandate, the goals of those who promoted Hebrew were Zionist goals, those of the Jewish national movement—the return of the Jewish people to its land and to normality. Hebrew was a central symbol for the awakening and maintenance of national sentiment. The promotion of Hebrew was a reminder of the glorious tradition connecting the Jewish people to its ancestors, and a sign of the national self-determination that they could win again. In principle, any common language can serve to mobilize the masses, but an indigenous language, carrier of a great classical, religious, and historical tradition, is an eminently powerful symbol around which to rally.

Once the ascendancy of Hebrew as the chief Jewish lingua franca in Palestine had been assured, there was a change in emphasis in the national goals served by the promotion of Hebrew. A vehicle of mass communication was needed to integrate the diverse ethnic groups making up the new nation, especially after the mass immigration that followed independence, and to facilitate the working of national institutions. This is not to say that Hebrew lost its role as a symbol of national identity—indeed, one could argue that it grew in symbolic value as the population became more diverse ethnolinguistically—but that those efforts originally directed towards exploiting the symbolic value of Hebrew, in order to mobilize the Jews in their struggle for self-determination, were redirected, once the struggle had been won, towards strengthening the position of Hebrew as a language of mass communication, in order to integrate and control a diverse population. The initial objectives of language planning were channelled chiefly towards modernizing Hebrew and encouraging people to use it; subsequent objectives were focused mainly on encouraging people to learn it.

As for the motivation of potential adopters of Hebrew, it is sometimes claimed that instrumental considerations were paramount in the case of immigrants who arrived after independence, but that, in contrast, ideological motivations were paramount in the early days of the revival movement. Certainly, the relationship that was discussed earlier between participation in the work-force and knowledge and use of Hebrew suggests the contemporary importance of material incentives in the adoption of Hebrew. It is also true that the immigrants who came to Palestine in the late nineteenth and early twentieth centuries were different from those who came later. Those who arrived before 1930 tended to be younger, with a better Jewish education and, therefore, greater prior knowledge of at least Hebrew, and with a much stronger commitment to Zionist ideology than those who came thereafter. Thus, the idea of reviving Hebrew as the chief language of everyday life among the Jews in the new settlements of Palestine was fully consistent both with their national aspirations and with their previous education. Certainly, the task of revival and revitalization was not easy: it was not just changes in language practice that were needed, but also changes in the language to deal with the requirements of everyday life (Rabin 1973: 72). Clearly, a strong ideological commitment was an essential component of Hebrew revitalization. At the same time, it must be noted, the increasing linguistic heterogeneity of the growing Jewish population clearly demanded a lingua franca, and Hebrew was the natural and logical choice for this purpose. Natural and logical in hindsight, perhaps, for most Jewish men and many women at that time had the benefit of a religious education which made them familiar with Hebrew, at least in its written forms. Any of the other competing possibilities—Yiddish, Arabic, German, French, Judezmo—would have had to be learned by a substantial portion of the population. And, of course, Hebrew did not have the more particular communal association of the other languages, symbolizing, as it did, the great tradition common to all Jews.

6

The Language of Signs

THE aim of this chapter and the next is to explore the form and nature of a theory of language choice, looking in particular at the suitability of a preference model for this purpose. In developing a tentative model, this chapter will present a set of rules accounting for the choice of language on public signs in the Old City; the next chapter will consider the rules of language choice as demonstrated by the speech of passers-by and shopkeepers in the streets of the market.

Our goal was to find the most parsimonious set of rules to account for the facts observed. Developed originally by Jackendoff for semantics, the preference model assumes that the rules that constitute a system need not all be 'necessary' conditions, that is, rules that apply without exception. Rules of the necessary kind are the basis of much of generative grammar; an ungrammatical sentence is the result of not following such a rule. But in the preference model there are other kinds of rules. Many of them are not binary (true or false) rules, but they establish gradient conditions instead, so that the more the condition described is true, the more likely the result is to be realized; in other words, they state probabilities and the conditions that control them. Gradient conditions set up probabilities of occurrence rather than describe absolute choices. A particularly important type of rule in a preference model is what is called a 'typicality' condition: the rule describes the typical or preferred state of affairs, but is not always true. What is significant about typicality conditions is that a system may easily contain two contradictory conditions; varying ideologies or situations will often account for the weighting given to each, and so explain the probable outcome in a specific case. Rules of this kind, it has been argued, underlie many aspects of human behaviour: they have been shown to be relevant to the analysis of semantics (Jackendoff), music (Lerdahl and Jackendoff), literature (Schauber and E. Spolsky), public worship (B. Spolsky and Walters), and second-language learning (B. Spolsky, Rutherford). This is the model that will be considered in this chapter and the next.

The language of the signs

Before looking at the underlying system, a question needs to be asked about the language of the signs (Table 6.1 lists all the signs discussed in this chapter). In most cases it is easy enough to decide in which language a sign is written. But there is a special problem with the street signs (see figs. 1.3, 1.4). Is the third language on the street signs in fact English? In the case of the 'HA-MALAKH RD.' sign, both the word order and the abbreviated word 'RD.' (road) suggest that the answer should be affirmative. Transliteration rather than translation is one common way of handling a non-European language in the European alphabet: other examples are:

OMAR IBN EL-KHATTAB SQ. (transliteration of the Arabic).

QABAT KHAN EL-AQBAT (transliteration of the Arabic; the added Hebrew name is 'RECHOV HAKOPTIM', 'Street of the Copts').

BAB EL-JADID RD. (transliteration of the Arabic; the added Hebrew is a translation, 'RECHOV SHA'AR HACHADASH', 'New Gate Road').

HABAD RD. (transliteration of the Hebrew).

One can argue that a transliterated name plus the English word 'road' or 'street' is at least in an English frame, but when the word for 'street' (*rechov*) is also in Hebrew, it is hard to argue that that is English. Occasionally, however, there is a translation rather than a transliteration:

WESTERN WALL RD.

ARMENIAN ORTHODOX PATRIARCHATE RD.

DAVID STREET

ST. FRANCIS RD.

CASA NOVA RD.

FRERES ROAD

The last two signs provide examples of a tendency to apply a non-English-based norm to the process of transliteration, as they follow the Latin and French spelling of the names of the buildings that have given their names to the streets. Freres Road, it will be noted, is named for the Collège de Frères; the Hebrew text on the sign is 'RECHOV HA-ACHIM', 'Street of the Brothers'. An interesting case is the sign 'ST GIRGES RD.'. The Latin characters are a partial transliteration of the Arabic; the added Hebrew is a transliteration of the English name 'St George's Rd.'.

The non-English forms produced by such transliteration make it appealing to consider the transliterated language on the street signs to be *loazit*, a general Hebrew term for foreign languages, also used to refer to something written in Latin characters; we might then choose to reserve the term 'English' for translated signs. However, the use of the English word 'road' or 'street' and the word order make clear that these street signs are in what Strevens (1978) calls a 'localized form' of English, differentiated in this case from Standard English by the use of transliteration or of other languages.

There are a number of other interesting questions to be raised about the actual content and linguistic form of the signs. Some of these points are concerned with translation or comparative stylistics (the provision of an explanation in one language but not another, for instance: the English of a 'NO PARKING' sign bears those words only, while the Arabic adds 'PRIVATE PROPERTY'); others, that will be touched on later, concern errors in one or more of the languages. However, this chapter will generally eschew the opportunuity for this finer analysis, concentrating instead on the question of language choice itself: what language or languages, and in what order, appear on the signs, and how can this choice be explained?

Taxonomies

Chapter 1 discussed briefly some of the signs encountered on a walk into the Old City. Just over 100 other signs have been recorded; Table 6.1 provides a list of them.[1]

A simple taxonomy, based on the function and use of the signs, will give some notion of the surface complexity: two types of sign were mentioned in Chapter 1, street signs and advertising placards; a third important classification is a sign designating the owner or purpose of a building or part of a building; a fourth is a warning or instruction. Altogether, eight major types of signs can usefully be distinguished.

1. Street signs
   (a) Tiled: pre-1948; pre-1948 amended after 1967; after 1967
   Examples of these have been discussed earlier. The street signs of the Old City are intended to be read by pedestrians (vehicular traffic is restricted), and the trilingual ceramic tiles are special to the Old City itself.
   (b) Other
   For example, the trilingual illuminated street sign (25).

2. Advertising signs
   (a) Locally prepared
   The 'NAMES' sign is one example (35); another is a menu outside a restaurant (22).
   (b) Nationally prepared
   For example, the 'KENT' cigarette posters, one in English and Arabic (15), and one in English and Hebrew (37); their difference in date is also apparent.
   (c) Internationally prepared
   For example, the 'KODAK' sign (101) and the bank-card symbols on the window of the jewellery shop (102).

3. Warning notices, prohibitions
   (a) Standard: official
   For example, the electricity warning (5) and the traffic sign (30).
   (b) Locally prepared

---

[1] This table lists the photographs which I took of signs in the Old City, only a few of which have been reproduced in this book. Some photographs show more than 1 sign; where this is so, the number is repeated. The numbering system is based on rolls of film: the first is 1–37; the second 101–37; and so on.

TABLE 6.1. *List of photographs of signs*

No.	Photograph	Languages			Material
2	Ha-Malakh Road	H	A	E	tile
3	El-Malak Road	A	E		tile
4	Benevolent Union	Arm.	A	E	painted board
5	Danger (electricity)	A	H	E	painted on metal
6	*Yishuv* museum	H	E		painted on metal
6	To the Maison	H	Fr.		painted on metal
7	Maison	H	Fr.	E	painted on metal
8	Name on letter-box	H	Fr.		marker on metal
9	Plaque on building	Arm.			engraved on stone
10	Announcement of films	Arm.			typed on paper
11	Armenian convent	Arm.	A	Fr.	painted on stone
12	Armenian museum	Arm.			tile
12	To the Armenian museum	E			painted board
15	Kent advertisement	A	E		poster
16	Restaurant sign	A	E	H	painted board
17	Police station	H	A	E	painted on glass
18	Post office	H	Fr.		painted on metal
19	Bank Leumi	H	E		painted board
20	Post office hours	H	A	E	painted board
21	Anglican church hours	E			painted board
21	Anglican church sign	E	H	A	painted board
22	Restaurant menu	E			painted board
23	Former Austrian PO	E	Germ.		engraved on stone
24	Christian Centre	E			painted board
25	To Western Wall	H	A	E	painted on metal
25	Boulos	A	E		painted board
27	Jaffa Gate	E	A	H	tile
28	Jaffa Gate	A			engraved on stone
28	Jaffa Gate	H			engraved on stone
30	Traffic sign	H			painted on metal
30	Traffic sign	H	A		painted on metal
31	Police call-box	H			metal
32	Christmas 1979	E			typed on paper
33	Christmas trees	H	A	E	typed on paper
34	Restaurant sign	A	E	H	painted board
35	Names made here	E			painted on metal
36	Souvenirs	E			painted board
36	Ice-cream	H			painted board
37	Kent advertisement	H	E		poster
101	Kodak advertisement outside Petra Hotel	E			painted board
102	Jewellery shop	E			painted board
103	To Nazarene church	A	E	Aram.	painted board

No.	Photograph	Languages	Material
104	St John's convent	Gk. E	engraved on stone
105	For visitors	Gk. E A	printed paper
106	*Nouveauté* shop	Fr. A	painted board
107	Artin shop	A E Arm.	painted board
108	Graffiti	A	painted on wall
109	Holy place	E	painted on wall
110	Greek convent	Gk.	painted board
113	Greek convent	Gk. A	painted board
114	Collège de Sainte Terre	Fr. A	painted board
115	Greek patriarchate	A Fr.	tile
116	Greek bookstore	Fr. E Germ.	paper
117	Greek church hours	Fr.	paper
118	No parking	E	painted board
119	St Vincent	It. A	painted board
123	Mission library	7 languages	paper
124	Latin patriarchate	Lat. A	painted board
125	Printer	A E H	painted board
126	Orphanage	Lat.	engraved on stone
127	For prayers only	A E	painted board
127	Mosque	A E	painted board
129	Hospice	Germ.	engraved on stone
130	Contractor	H	painted board
132	Contractor	E	painted board
133	Station of Cross	E Germ.	painted board
135	Coptic patriarchate	Cop. A E	painted board
136	Block-number	H	painted board
202	Kodak (on Agfa)	E A	marker on metal
203	Barber	A E	painted board
204	Hostel	E Swed.	painted board
205	Postal agency	H A Fr.	painted on metal
208	Western Wall rules	H Fr. E	painted board
209	To Jaffa Gate	H A. Fr. E	painted board
230	Army post	H	painted board
232	Mosque area hours	E	painted on metal
234	Khalidi shop	A E	painted board
235	T-shirts	E H A	cloth
301	Public conveniences	H A E	painted on glass
302	Danger (electricity)	H E A	painted on metal
302	Danger (electricity)	A H E	painted on metal
303	Announcement	H	paper
304	Wohl Centre	H E	metal letters
305	Hospice	H E	engraved on stone
306	Postal agency	H A E	painted on glass
307	Postal agency hours	H	painted on metal

No.	Photograph	Languages				Material
308	Token machine	H				painted on metal
309	Assyrian Convent Road	H	A	E		tile
310	Assyrian Convent Road	H	A	E		tile
311	Assyrian Convent Road	H	A	E		tile
312	Assyrian convent	Aram.	H	A		mosaic
313	Assyrian convent	A	E			engraved on stone
314	Graffito	E				painted on wall
315	Anglican bookshop	E	H	A		painted board
316	Pages	E	H			paper
317	Anglican church	E	H	A		painted board
318	Post office	H	E	A		painted board
319	Post office hours	H	E	A		painted board
320	Letter-box	H				metal
321	Letter-box	E				metal
322	Restaurant menu	E	H	A		painted on wall
326	Restaurant sign	E				painted board
326	Garbage	H	A			painted board
327	Graffito					painted on wall
328	Courtyard	H	E			painted on metal
329	To walking-tour	E				painted board
330	Fruit shop	H				painted on glass
331	Danger (electricity)	A	H	E		painted on metal
332	Shop hours	E				painted board
334	Clinic	H				painted board
335	Notices	H				paper
336	Memorial	H				metal letters
337	Bank	H	A	E		metal letters
338	Police station	H	E			painted on glass
339	Bank	H	E			painted on glass

Note: Languages have been abbreviated as follows: H = Hebrew; A = Arabic; E = English; Arm. = Armenian; Fr. = French; Germ. = German; Aram. = Aramaic; Gk. = Greek; It. = Italian; Lat. = Latin; Cop. = Coptic; Swed. = Swedish.

Official

For example, 'VISITORS PLEASE RING THE BELL' (105), the Arabic–English 'NO PARKING' (118), and 'FOR PRAYERS ONLY' (127).

Private

For example, the 'HOLY PLACE' sign (109), which is probably to be interpreted as 'Keep out' or 'Do not urinate here'.

4. Building (part of building) names
   (*a*) Standard (official)
   For example, the trilingual (Hebrew, Arabic, English) sign on the police

station, 'POLICE' (17), or the bilingual (Hebrew, French) sign on the post office, 'POSTE' (18), and the more recent versions of these signs, bilingual on the police station in Hebrew and English, and trilingual on the post office in Hebrew, Arabic, and English.

(*b*) Institutional

For instance, the trilingual (English, Hebrew, Arabic) 'CHRIST CHURCH' (21), the monolingual English 'CHRISTIAN INFORMATION CENTRE' (24), the bilingual Greek–English 'ST JOHN'S CONVENT' (104), the trilingual (Armenian, Arabic, French) 'COUVENT ARMÉNIEN DE ST JACQUES' (11), the bilingual (Latin–Arabic) 'OFFICIUM PAROECIAE LATINAE JERUSALEM— CUSTODIA TERRA SANCTAE' (124), and the bilingual Arabic–English 'KHANQA SALAHIEH MOSQUE' (127).

(*c*) Commercial establishments

For example, the bilingual Hebrew–English 'BANK LEUMI LE' ISRAEL' (19), later replaced by a trilingual sign in Hebrew, English, and Arabic, the monolingual English 'PETRA HOTEL' (101), the trilingual (Arabic, Hebrew, English) 'ABOU SEIF RESTAURANT—ORIENTAL, TURKISH & PERSIAN DISHES' (34).

(*d*) Home

For example, the monolingual Hebrew block-number of a building (136), or the family names on letter-boxes (unnumbered).

5. Informative signs

   (*a*) Permanent

   Direction

   For example, 'OLD YISHUV COURT MUSEUM' (6), 'ARMENIAN MUSEUM' (12), 'TO THE WESTERN WALL' (25), 'TO THE JAFFA GATE' (209).

   Hours of opening

   For example, on the post office (20), in Hebrew, Arabic, and English (recall that the building sign was in Hebrew and French), and on Christ Church (21) in English (the building sign was in three languages).

   (*b*) Temporary or seasonal

   For example, posters (32, 108, 123).

6. Commemorative plaques

   For example, in English on the former Austrian post office (23), or in Arabic, Turkish, or Hebrew on the Jaffa Gate (28, 29).

7. Signs labelling objects

   For example, the monolingual Hebrew police call-box (31), or the old monolingual English letter-box (320).

8. Graffiti

   For example, the anti-Turkish signs that appear (usually in English) on walls around the Armenian quarter at about the date that serves to commemorate the massacres. One might also include under this heading the defacement of various signs (which sometimes includes vandalizing one of its languages (4).

Other taxonomies are possible. A second principle of classification that could be employed is one based on the material from which the sign is made, or its physical form. The types included then would cover the following:

1. Written with a marker or brush on any surface (108).
2. Typed or written on paper (33, 123).
3. Printed poster (32).
4. Painted sign on wooden board (36, 101, 110).
5. Illuminated (painted on glass or plastic) (17).
6. Painted sign on metal (127, 303).
7. Painted on a tile (2).
8. Bronze or metal (engraved or cut out) (31).
9. Engraved or embossed on stone (9, 126).

Position in the list has been determined more or less according to the permanence of the signs, and the degree of skill required to make them.

Classification by the language, or number of languages, of the sign (see Table 6.2) is a third potential taxonomy. Most of the signs in this study are in one, two, or three languages, as Table 6.3 demonstrates. The most common languages are Hebrew, English, and Arabic, but at least a dozen different ones were recorded overall; while impressive, this omits a significant number of the thirty or so languages that people in the Old City claim to speak. Two further taxonomic principles will be considered in the analysis below: the presumed language of the owner of the sign (that is, the owner of the building, or the person presumed to have erected the sign); and the probable language of the reader of the sign or of the user of the facility on which it appears.

Like all attempts at categorization, taxonomy cannot be expected to provide comprehensive answers to the questions that arise, or even to work unambiguously; some signs, for instance, fall into two or more groups, as when a sign giving the name of a commercial establishment goes on to advertise its wares or to inform of its hours. Moreover, a taxonomy is not an explanation; without further clarification, classifying a sign does not explain the language chosen. Some deeper analysis is needed; the rules that follow are both more abstract and more explanatory.

The rules of signs

The first rule proposed is a necessary condition for signs: the limitation of the sign to languages that the sign-writer knows:

Sign Rule 1 ('sign-writer's skill' condition—necessary, graded): write signs in a language you know.

TABLE 6.2 *Languages of signs*

1st language on sign	2nd language on sign	3rd language on sign	Frequency
A	—	—	2
A	E	—	10
A	E	H	3
A	E	Arm.	1
A	E	Aram.	1
A	Fr.	—	1
A	H	E	1
Aram.	H	A	1
Arm.	—	—	3
Arm.	A	E	1
Arm.	A	Fr.	1
Cop.	A	E	1
E	—	—	18
E	A	—	1
E	A	H	1
E	Germ.	—	2
E	H	—	1
E	H	A	5
E	Sw.	—	1
Fr.	—	—	1
Fr.	A	—	2
Fr.	E	—	1
Germ.	—	—	1
Gk.	—	—	1
Gk.	A	—	1
Gk.	E	—	2
H	—	—	15
H	A	E	14
H	A	—	2
H	E	—	9
H	E	A	2
H	Fr.	—	3
H	Fr.	E	1
It.	A	—	1
Lat.	—	—	1
Lat.	A	—	1

Note: For a list of abbreviations, see Table 6.1.

TABLE 6.3 *Summary of principal languages used on signs*

	Position on sign		
	Alone or 1st	2nd or 3rd	Total
Arabic	19	31	50
Hebrew	46	11	57
English	29	46	75

At first glance this seems to be too obvious to need stating, but it turns out to be useful for a number of reasons. First, it accounts for the restriction to English, Hebrew, and Arabic of most advertising signs. Second, it shows why, whenever possible, other tourist languages are used (the 'NAMES MADE HERE' sign appears in German, Dutch, and Swedish). Third, because it is a graded condition, it allows for various levels of language knowledge, and explains the errors in spelling, grammar, or vocabulary on many signs (most noticeably on menus). That is to say, a corollary of Sign Rule 1 is that a sign provides evidence of the extent of a sign-writer's knowledge of languages. Fourth, it deals in part with the interaction between medium and language: the more permanent the sign, the fewer languages it will use; the more difficult and permanent a sign, the more likely it is to have been made by an expert. It is then possible to seek a translation. But cost will limit the number of languages used on permanent signs (there are few with more than three); and engraved signs are generally monolingual.

While the sign-writer's skill condition is a necessary condition, it should be noted that it pertains to the language knowledge of the sign-writer and not to that of the owner or originator of the sign; in the case of professional signs, therefore, it does not indicate the literacy of the owner, but his choice of language as limited by the capabilities of the sign-writer. However, the rule does apply directly in the case of home-made, non-professional signs, especially graffiti.

To go beyond this first necessary condition, it is useful to start with the 'NAMES MADE HERE' sign (see Fig. 1.2). This was, it will be recalled, a monolingual sign advertising the shopkeeper's willingness to make silver or gold names in English, Arabic, or Hebrew. While this offer of trilingual jewellery would appear to be aimed at those people who read those three languages, the sign itself appeared in only one language; it was reasonable to assume, therefore, that it was intended to be read by people who knew that language, namely, foreign tourists. This suggests a second rule:

Sign Rule 2 ('presumed reader' condition—typical, graded): prefer to write signs in the language or languages that intended readers are assumed to read.

This rule applies particularly when the primary aim of the sign-writer is to convey information; the major motivation is likely to be economic.

The third rule is derivable from the case of the tiled street signs discussed in Chapter 1, the two forms of the 'HA-MALAKH RD' sign, and the related 'JAFFA GATE' sign (see Figs. 1.3, 1.4, 1.5). The explanation for the different forms, it was suggested, was that these street signs record clearly the recent history of the Old City. The sign on the Jaffa Gate dated from the British Mandate period, before 1948, which is why it was written in what were then the three official languages of the Mandate government: English first, Arabic second, and Hebrew third. The second sign chronologically was the expanded sign, the last two lines of which originally formed a complete sign put up during the Jordanian period, and which was therefore written in Arabic with an English transliteration. The Arabic script used was a clear, modern script, reflecting a growing level of literacy and the recognition of functional use (presumed reader condition). After 1967, when the Old City came under Israeli rule, this bilingual sign was modified by adding an extra line with the Hebrew name of the street printed on it; the Hebrew was put first in order. Since then, whenever new signs are needed, they are prepared in the same three languages: Hebrew first, Arabic second, and English third, the latter a transliteration of the Hebrew.

To handle this notion of official policy, where the decision is based not on the necessary condition or on the presumed readership but rather on the symbolic value of the language choice, I propose a third rule, as follows:

> Sign Rule 3 ('symbolic value' condition—typical, graded): prefer to write signs in your own language or in a language with which you wish to be identified.

This rule will cover both official and private decisions about language choice or order. For the tiles, it was symbolic value that decided that English, Arabic, and Hebrew each had their turn at the top of the list; it was symbolic value, too, that included a calligraphic Arabic in the Mandate period; symbolic value that omitted Hebrew in the period of Jordanian occupation; symbolic value that determined that the *loazit* on the Israeli signs should be based on the Hebrew rather than the Arabic street name. Just as language use can proclaim a speaker's regional origin or educational level, so the language of a sign can proclaim the language loyalty and values of the sign-writer. One expression of language-loyalty value is official language policy.

In the same way as the primary motivation of Sign Rule 2 (presumed reader condition) is likely to be economic, the primary motivation of Sign Rule 3 (symbolic value condition) is likely to be either political or socio-cultural. It derives its value, that is to say, from a desire to assert power (by controlling the languages of the sign, I declare power over the space designated) or to claim solidarity or identity (my statement of socio-cultural membership is in the language I have chosen).

How do these three rules work in practice? To start with, one might want to look at the language that appears first on a multilingual sign or alone on a monolingual one. In the majority of cases (fifty-three out of the ninety-one included in my study sample), the first or only language of the sign is the native language of the presumed owner of the premises or of the person who put up the sign. In most of these cases, however, it is to be noted that the first or only language of the sign is also the language of the presumed reader or user. In other words, in about half of the cases, all three rules apply. In some models this would be called over-determination. In a preference model it is said to lead to a strong judgement; these signs are the ones that are 'obviously' in the right language.

That leaves a small but interesting group of signs where the symbolic value condition applies but not the presumed reader condition, cases where proclaiming ownership is more important than being understood. All but one of these are signs on buildings owned by institutions (114 in French, 124 and 126 in Latin, 104, 113, and 129 in Greek, 135 in Coptic, and 129 in German).

In about a third of the cases, the presumed reader condition applies in contradiction to the symbolic value or owner's condition. Most of these are commercial signs (advertisements, shop names, signs for tourists), where the need to accommodate is strongest: when the goal is to sell, it is obvious that the language of the buyer is most important. This is illustrated clearly by two shops selling women's clothing in the Jewish quarter; one, catering to tourists, has its signs in Hebrew and English; the second, wishing to serve Jewish Israelis only, has a sign in Hebrew alone. We will find the same kind of accommodation when we come to consider speech in the market-place.

Applying the rules

Within the framework provided by these three rules, a number of questions may now be explored. The spoken languages of the market in the Old City are (in order of frequency) Arabic, Hebrew, English, and other languages. First, why are all advertising signs not in at least the first three languages? There are a number of contributory factors. First, internationally prepared advertising signs ('KODAK' in 101, or the bank-card symbols on the window in 102) are provided to the shopkeeper ready-made, in the international version in appropriate Roman characters. Occasionally, special national versions are prepared (on a monolingual Arabic 'AGFA FILM' sign (202) the shopkeeper has been constrained to print in English 'WE SELL KODAK FILM'), but the decision is not up to the shopkeeper, so that the sign might not represent his presumptions. This is also true of nationally prepared signs like the two 'KENT' cigarette signs, one for Israel (see Fig. 6.1; note that the pack depicted is in English, but the Hebrew is added to the poster), and one for Arab countries (see Fig. 6.2) with Arabic added to the English pack. For this reason, a sign might not be accurately targeted at the intended local population; occasionally (as in the 'AGFA' sign), the shopkeeper will then make a change.

FIG. 6.1. *'Kent' Hebrew poster*

A second reason why advertising signs in the Old City are not written in at least the three main languages is the variation in the utilization of signs according to the shopping habits of the various groups. Arabs shopping in the markets of the Old City buy either non-advertised items (fruit and vegetables, spices) or imported items in labelled boxes; any advertising matter on display will have been provided by the manufacturer or his agent, although it should be noted that, in recent months, longer hand-written advertisements in Arabic have been starting to appear, suggesting an increase in literacy skills. The shopkeepers do not seem to aim to attract these customers with specially prepared signs, but with a careful and attractive display of objects. Nor are prices generally displayed, for this remains a bargaining market. Israeli Jews, too, are assumed to be able to find what they are after without a special written message. So, locally prepared advertising signs would appear on the whole to be intended for foreign tourists.

Why then are the signs not written in more languages? The answer is twofold: the first, following the sign-writer's skill condition, is the limitation of signs to languages that the writer knows; the second, following the presumed reader condition, is the assumption that English is the tourist language of wider communication and will reach the largest possible readership. One notes that the prices occasionally marked on fruit and vegetables (a practice that has become standard in recent years in the fruit and vegetable market in West Jerusalem), are written not in Arabic but in European (so-called) numerals. Arabs assume that they will bargain when making such purchases; Europeans will often not understand the statement of the price unless it is written for them.

It is interesting to see how these rules apply to some of the types of signs classified earlier.

FIG. 6.2. *'Kent' Arabic poster*

Warning notices and prohibitions

The electricity 'DANGER' sign (5) is in three languages: Arabic first, then Hebrew and English. One might immediately consider this to be a direct application of the presumed reader condition—that signs are written in the most appropriate language for the addressees. Thus, it might be argued that the sign-writer assumed that most people would read Arabic, followed by Hebrew and English in that order. But when one knows that the sign was put up by the East Jerusalem Electric Company, which is under Arab control, then there is good reason to suspect some other explanation as well, and therefore to postulate the symbolic value condition as an additional explanation. The change to the Israeli grid involved changes in these signs, with the order of languages becoming Hebrew, Arabic, and English: the two can sometimes be seen side by side (see Fig. 6.3).

FIG. 6.3. *Electric Company warning signs*

Official policy is one expression of language loyalty; official signs, however, might also simply assume a certain readership. This becomes most obvious with standard signs, such as the traffic and parking notices (30) in the Old City. Here there are two signs on the same post: one sets a weight limit on vehicles, and is in Hebrew and Arabic; the other lists exceptions (which includes not just obvious Hebrew readers—the army, the police, ambulances, and the fire brigade—but probable non-Hebrew readers—the United Nations and diplomats) to this restriction in Hebrew only.

Normally, however, one would expect the presumed reader condition to be the most important rule for warning signs; a sign at the entrance to the Western Wall plaza provides an interesting illustration of this (see Fig. 6.4). This sign is written in three languages: first Hebrew, then French, and then English. The simplest explanation for the absence of Arabic (and many Arabs do cross the Western Wall plaza on their way to and from the village of Silwan outside the Dung Gate) is that Arabs do not dress immodestly: Arab men do not wear shorts, nor do Arab women go about with their shoulders uncovered. Supporting this interpretation is the fact that, in the same area, there is a sign to the Jaffa Gate which is written in four languages—Hebrew, French, Arabic, and English.

There is another possible interpretation, a kind of negative application of the symbolic value condition, which takes the form: prefer not to use a language with which you do not wish to be identified. This might be a better explanation of the fact that there is a sign on a Greek church asking visitors to ring the bell (see Fig. 6.5) which is in Greek, English, and Arabic but not Hebrew, even though there are many Hebrew-reading tourists, or why the sign barring tourists (it reads 'FOR PRAYERS ONLY') on the Khanqa Salahieh mosque is in Arabic and English only. The former might well be considered to represent a written continuation of the policy of discouraging Jews from entering the Christian quarter (see Ben-Arieh 1984: 377.)

This negative rule also accounts for a tendency to deface signs by making one or more of the languages on a multilingual sign illegible: the vandal is proclaiming the illegitimacy of that particular language for public display.

Names on buildings, institutions, and shops

Names on buildings, institutions, commercial establishments, and homes probably demonstrate the greatest variety in languages, reflecting the fact that, of all signs, they are more likely to conform to the symbolic value condition. One would normally expect the first language used to be the native language of the owner or occupier, who uses the sign to proclaim identity, and this is generally the case:

Armenian on the sign for the Jerusalem Armenian Benevolent Union (4).

Hebrew on signs for the police (17), the post office (18), or the bank (19); letter-boxes in the Jewish quarter, a contractor's noticeboard on improvements in the

FIG. 6.4. *Request for modest dress*

FIG. 6.5. *Sign for visitors*

Christian quarter (130), and an army post (230; the building in which the post is located has an Arabic inscription in the lintel stone).

Arabic on the mosque (128) and on Arab-owned shops (34) (note that an Armenian-owned shop (2) uses English).

English on Christ Church (21) and the Christian Information Centre (24).

Greek on St John's convent (104).

French on the Collège de Terre Sainte (114).

Latin on the sign for the Society of St Vincent de Paul (119), and on Franciscan buildings (126).

German on the St John's hospice (129).

Swedish (but one word only) on the Mid-City Swedish Youth Hostel (204; perhaps it is *for* Swedes rather than owned by them).

However, the simultaneous operation of the presumed reader condition can be seen in the large number of these signs that also include a second or third language, enabling a chosen fraction of the passers-by to understand the sign.

Informative signs

For informative signs, as with warning signs, one would expect the presumed reader condition to be the most significant. For example, whereas the identifying sign on the post office (18) used to be in Hebrew and French (the latter a reminder of the period when the Israeli government, shortly after independence, was looking for reasons to downgrade English; the post office rushed to follow the policy of the Union Postale Universelle and use French), the hours of opening are in the more useful Hebrew, Arabic, and English (20). Direction signs at the Western Wall are in Hebrew, Arabic, French, and English. The extensive signposting for tourists in the Jewish quarter is in Hebrew and English. An English and German sign on a station of the Cross makes clear for which tourists it is intended. A poster giving information on Christmas services in Nazareth (32) is in English. A notice issued by the Jerusalem municipality giving information on the distribution of free Christmas trees (33) applies the symbolic value condition by putting the Hebrew text before the Arabic and English ones.

Commemorative plaques

By their nature, commemorative plaques are most likely to give priority to the symbolic value condition, so that their language can reinforce the ownership claimed by the plaque. This is true of the Arabic and Hebrew plaques on the Jaffa Gate (28). But commemorative plaques, too, sometimes have translations, and in the case of the old Austrian post office (see Fig. 6.6), the bulk of the sign is an English translation.

FIG. 6.6. *Austrian post office plaque*

The Police signs

A particularly interesting example here is the call-box used by the police (31), which has on it the police symbol (a star with the Hebrew letter 'mem') and the word for 'police' in Hebrew. This contrasts with the police station itself, which until recently was identified in three languages. In each case, the dominant rules appeared to be the presumed reader condition, for it seemed to be assumed that all policemen—Jews, Arabs, or Druse—could read Hebrew, but that the general public needed the three languages. However, new signs have appeared in the police station in the last year or so in two languages only, Hebrew and English. The significance of this change will be discussed in Chapter 8.

Graffiti

Graffiti are written first and foremost in the language of the originator; they are, in other words, governed primarily by the sign-writer's skill condition. But if they have an informative function, the presumed reader condition becomes important; graffiti that appear on the walls of the Armenian quarter to mark the anniversary of the massacres (and that are whitewashed a week or so later) tend, therefore, to be in English. A particularly striking manifestation of this are the occasional attempts to apply a reverse version of the symbolic value condition by erasing one

FIG. 6.7. *Defaced Armenian sign*

FIG. 6.8. *Defaced street sign*

of the languages of a sign: this is to be noted with the defacing of the Arabic in the Armenian sign (see Fig. 6.7), which pre-dates 1980. The Arabic on a number of street signs in the Jewish quarter was painted over in about 1984; some were cleaned up later, but others remain (see Fig. 6.8). At the same time, an attempt was made to chip away the letters of the word 'German' which was written in Hebrew and English on an archaeological remain in the Jewish quarter.

To conclude: it is possible to explain the language chosen for signs in the Old City by postulating three rules. The first of these is a necessary condition: write signs in a language you know. The other two are typicality conditions, and, as such, are often in conflict. One of them is concerned with the directly informative nature of a sign, preferring to use a language which accords with the writer's assumption of the literacy of the desired or potential reader. The other is concerned with the symbolic (or political or other) value of the language being used; it proclaims ownership, as it were, by using the writer's own or preferred language and by showing his or her claim to identity. Sign Rule 1 is the practical limitation; Sign Rule 2 is concerned with the instrumental or pragmatic use of the sign—where the emphasis is to be on the content; Sign Rule 3 involves the expression of a more affective value—where the choice of language is itself the message. In any specific case, the inherent function of the sign will predict which of these two rules applies first and whether the other rule is to be allowed its place, too, producing a multilingual sign.

7

Language Choice in the Market-Place

ONE of the central issues in the study of multilingual communities is the recognition of the 'variables which may contribute to an understanding of *who* speaks *what* language to *whom* and *when*' (Fishman 1971: 583). Fishman believes that by establishing the factors involved in stable multilingual situations, it should be easier to understand less stable situations. One such variable that helps to elucidate what happens in stable multilingual communities is the higher-order construct of 'domain'.

Fishman maintained that in a speech community like the Jersey City barrio, with its use of two languages, Spanish and English, the choice between these two languages can be accounted for in this way. A domain is defined, he says, 'in terms of *institutional contexts and their congruent behavioral co-occurrences*' (1971: 586); it is a 'higher-order generalization from *congruent situations*' where role-relationship, topic, and locale all agree (ibid. 589). One such domain in the Jersey City study was the family (with role-relationships like father–child, topics like food, and the home serving as locale); another was work (with role-relationships like employer–employee, and congruent topics and locales): the family domain is generally associated with Spanish, the work domain with English.

In less stable situations, such as immigrant-host relations or contact between speech communities, domains are likely to be more restricted. The model assumed by Fishman is that these higher-order, socially determined factors will establish overall patterns, but there will be room for individual 'interpersonal fluctuation' within these (1971: 585).

The market-place, as Cooper and Carpenter (1976: 254) remarked, is a promising context for the study of language choice: it permits surveys in situations where more detailed household studies are not feasible, and makes it possible to check actual usage against reported claims. This chapter will explore the rules underlying language choice in the market-place of the Old City of Jerusalem; as in the previous chapter, the goal is to find the most parsimonious set of rules to account for what was observed.

To start with, two rules are posited, analogues of those developed to account for the language of signs. The first of these rules is the necessary condition of knowing a language before you use it; the second is a typicality condition—the use, whenever possible, of a language presumed to be intelligible to the addressee. Just as these were relevant to an explanation of the language of signs, they underlie also the choice of spoken language, but there are extra complexities to be dealt with here.

A critical feature to note is that, given the existence of sufficiently important other reasons, a speaker can modify his or her language knowledge by learning another language. Let us consider a hypothetical example: if a person regularly buys food from a seller whose native language is different from his own, he or she may well be willing to learn the necessary few words or phrases to facilitate this regular transaction, but, as this custom is important to the merchant, there is greater practical pressure on him to learn the customer's language. Cooper and Carpenter (1976) showed the effect of this principle in the Ethiopian markets, and it is further demonstrated in the markets of the Old City of Jerusalem.

In this simple model, a single pressure, the instrumental need for communication between speakers of two different languages, will account for changes in proficiency, and so in the working of these first two rules. A further dimension is added when the language choice is related to a wider context (for example, one language is politically or socially dominant, the other language is that of a dominated group), or when the social relation itself is valued as much as the practical business (for example, the participants are trying to be good neighbours or fellow citizens as well as seller and buyer). And for either party, the need to learn a new language is, as Guiora and Acton (1979) suggested, a challenging of personal identity, so that this will be added to the complex model explaining whether or not the cost of language learning will be considered worthwhile.

It seems useful at this point to posit a set of norms for language choice, themselves best represented by a set of preference rules consisting, as defined in the last chapter, of some minimum set of necessary conditions, and in addition other rules that apply typically but not necessarily, the weighting or salience of which is dependent on situations and attitudes. This chapter will explore the application of these rules to the data in the market-place study, and then consider possible modifications.

Choosing a language you know

Chapter 6 established the first rule governing the choice of language for a sign as being:

Sign Rule 1 (sign-writer's skill condition—necessary, graded): write signs in a language you know.

The rule, it was noted, applied to the sign-writer rather than to the sign-owner; by being a graded condition, it accounted for errors in the language of signs; but it otherwise set a necessary condition for language choice in signs. A similar first rule governs language choice in speech:

Language Choice Rule 1 (knowledge condition—necessary, graded): use (speak, write) a language you know.

To what extent does the knowledge condition account for language use in the streets of the market-place in the Old City? The data for this survey were collected by nine pairs of Bar-Ilan University students as part of their work for a course in socio-linguistics. Each pair followed the same route through the main streets of the Old City; most of the streets are lined by shops and stalls, and there is heavy pedestrian traffic when the market is open. The pairs worked to identical instructions: while walking along the predetermined route, they were to make a note of the age and appearance of speakers, and the place, time, and language of at least twenty conversations in each of nine geographically defined sectors (see Fig. 7.1).

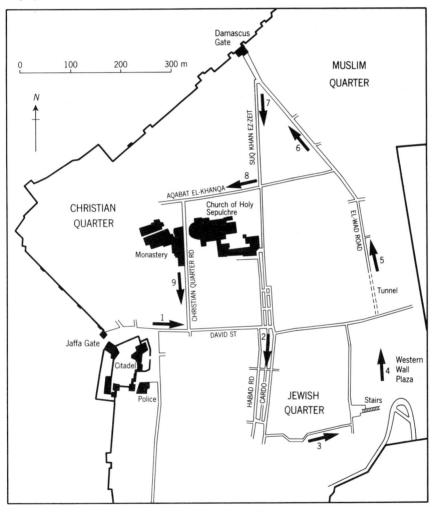

FIG. 7.1. *Route for language observation survey*

The largest number of transactions were recorded as being in Arabic (549), followed by Hebrew (430) and English (375); these three principal languages accounted for about three-quarters of the total. German and French occurred in significant numbers; the Scandinavian languages and Greek, Yiddish, and Spanish also appeared regularly. It is important to note that only some of the people observed were in fact residents of the Old City: whereas nearly 90 per cent of Old City residents are Arabs, less than 40 per cent of those recorded in the street survey were Arabs. The tourists (who made up about 30 per cent of those observed) and many of the Israeli Jews (20 per cent of those observed) were visitors to the Old City. It is by correlating the appearance and language choice of participants that the effect of the knowledge condition on language choice can be seen. The results are summarized below.

Palestinians, whether dressed in traditional village garb or in modern Western clothes, were most likely to use Arabic; the former were occasionally observed using Hebrew, and the latter using Hebrew, English, and other languages. Israeli Jews used Hebrew on the whole, but a proportion (14 per cent) was observed using English (some of them were working in the stores in the Cardo, a restored Byzantine street in the Jewish quarter), and 5 per cent were observed using Arabic, many of them presumably in transactions with merchants. Ultra-Orthodox Jews were not observed using Arabic (although, as noted in Chapter 2, many former residents of the Old City know the language); their observed use of Hebrew was quite low, and they generally seemed to communicate in either Yiddish or English. People wearing Christian clerical garb (priests, nuns, etc.) did not use Hebrew, but local Christian clergymen do know Arabic (18 per cent were observed to use it). The policemen in the Old City are mainly Arabs, and 46 per cent of the transactions involving them were in Arabic; the same proportion was in Hebrew; a few were noticed using English, presumably with tourists. The Israeli soldiers mainly used Hebrew, but some used Arabic, and some English. Those who appeared to be tourists were marked by their low level of use of the two local languages; they used other languages most of the time, and English as a lingua franca.

The overall picture is clear and obvious: Palestinians use Arabic; Israeli Jews and soldiers use Hebrew; tourists use English or other languages; Christian clerics use other languages; ultra-Orthodox Jews use Yiddish or English; and policemen (many of whom are Palestinians) use Arabic and Hebrew. These conclusions agree with the results of the language census, in which a third of the adult Arabic-speakers claimed also to be able to speak Hebrew, and nearly half to be able to speak English; their knowledge of Hebrew and English explains the fact that about a quarter of the native speakers of Arabic was observed in transactions using a language other than Arabic.

Tourists provide another excellent illustration of the application of the know-ledge condition. Not knowing the two major local languages, Hebrew or Arabic, tourists use either their native language or a second language, namely, English.

Similarly, the low percentage of local Jews observed using Arabic is in large measure a result of their lack of knowledge of that language. The high level of use of English by Arab traders is partly a reflection of their ignorance of tourists' other native languages, but it can also be explained by the fact that tourists will often assume that English is the best choice, given that their own language is not likely to be understood by the trader. Traders in the market can often be observed guessing a passer-by's language and offering a greeting in it.

The fact that language use does not accord completely with appearance and knowledge is evidence of two facts: one, that there exist bilinguals and multi-linguals; and, second, that there are circumstances under which people are ready to use a second language. The most obvious of these circumstances is considered in the next section, which examines the use of the language of one's interlocutor.

Choosing a language that will be understood

The second rule for the language of signs was the presumed reader rule, the choice of a language presumed to be understood by the person for whom the sign is intended. In the case of signs, there is no obvious immediate way to check the correctness of the decision; in the case of face-to-face communication, however, the existence (or absence) of feedback means that the rule can be applied more than once, and that corrections can be made when it is found that the first choice was wrong. The rule can be formulated as follows:

Language Choice Rule 2 (communication condition—necessary, graded): use (speak, write) a language presumed to be understood by the person with whom you wish to communicate.

While it is true that knowing a language is a graded condition—that is to say, that one's knowledge of a language can be measured on a number of dimensions—a necessary condition for a well-formed linguistic interaction is that the speaker and the hearer must have reached a certain minimal level of knowledge to make communication between them possible.

These first two conditions explain why it is that one of the first tasks that parents accept with a new-born child is to teach it their language, i.e. to make sure that it can meet the communication condition. Similarly, these two conditions explain why the continued presence of a significant monolingual in the home (say, an elderly grandparent or a newly arrived immigrant uncle or aunt) will ensure that other members of the family will know that language. In communicating with oneself (counting, dreaming, writing notes), it is obvious that the speaker/writer has the fullest freedom.

In a multilingual situation, appearance is a good first criterion for determining language choice with a stranger. Clothing is often distinctive—the uniforms of soldiers and policemen, the recognizable garb of the various clergy, the robes of the village Arabs, the black suits and hats of the ultra-Orthodox Jews, the knitted *kippot* (skull-caps) of modern Orthodox Israelis, the cameras and very short shorts of foreign tourists—all make it easy to guess the probable language knowledge of a stranger. Table 7.1, which presents cross-tabulations between appearance and observed language use, can help us understand choices in the Old City market-place. Assuming one knows the language (knowledge condition), it is an obvious first guess, in order to meet the communication condition, to start by speaking Arabic to a local or village Arab, Hebrew to an Israeli Jew or soldier, Hebrew or Yiddish to an ultra-Orthodox Jew. It is also likely to be a good bet to speak English to a tourist, although with greater skill it is possible to recognize, and so address correctly, the various national groups. Watching small boys trying to peddle postcards, or shopkeepers trying to tempt passers-by to enter their shops, one realizes why market traders place such a high value on being able to identify an interlocutor's language.

TABLE 7.1. *Cross-Tabulation (from observations) of language and appearance*

Appearance	Language			
	Arabic	English	Hebrew	Other
Town Arabs	384	62	50	28
Village Arabs	100	6	14	4
Clerics	10	12	0	33
Tourists	5	207	14	250
Israeli Jews	17	54	275	29
Ultra-Orthodox Jews	0	7	22	30
Police	6	1	6	0
Soldiers	4	5	21	2

Chapter 6 suggested that the primary motivation for the presumed reader or communication condition is in fact economic. Economic pressures play a major part in determining language use in a multilingual world. These first two necessary rules, then, help to explain the language of the commercial transactions between traders and tourists. The survey analysed transactions conducted inside a shop separately; they were usually, but not always, observed from outside. About a fifth (307) of the total observations were of encounters inside shops, and half of these (177) were inside shops that catered to tourists. In the latter case, the fact that the transactions were conducted inside had a clear effect on language choice, with two-thirds of the conversations taking place in English and other tourist languages. With regard to those shops serving mainly local residents (e.g. selling food or hardware), more than half of the transactions were in Arabic or

Hebrew. Given that most of the shopkeepers in the *shuk* are Arabs or Armenians, and that in the Cardo and the rest of the Jewish quarter they are Jews, this is good evidence of accommodation—the shopkeepers are seen to use a non-native language in order to suit their customers.

It is also possible to look at the data from the point of view of roles rather than location, and consider the language choice of buyers and sellers. While the majority of sellers were native speakers of Arabic or Armenian, they were more likely to use a language other than Arabic: they were also more likely to be addressed in a language other than Arabic. But there was an interesting difference: whereas the sellers used Arabic 223 times and other languages 333 times, they were spoken to in Arabic 175 times and in other languages 215 times. There is a hint here that some buyers might also have been making an effort at accommodation.

The first interpretation of these data, based only on the knowledge condition and the communication condition, must be that, because Arabic-speaking traders are more likely to know Hebrew than tourists or Israeli Jews are to know Arabic, pragmatically, these two necessary conditions explain language choice. They make clear why a bilingual speaking to a monolingual chooses to use the monolingual's language. With these two necessary conditions in place (and noting the effect of the inertia condition, to be discussed in more detail below), we have to consider another possibility, namely, the absence of a common language, before we can move on to look at the rules governing those situations where both participants are bilingual.

The absence of shared languages

In the eighteenth and nineteenth centuries the lack of linguistic skills on the part of Ashkenazic Jews, the fact that they had not learned Arabic, was given as a reason for their continuing poverty. The establishment of routine commercial transactions, however, ensured increased language knowledge; just as Arabs in the earlier periods were reported to have learned Judezmo, so they now came to know Yiddish. But this language knowledge was not itself critical for buying and selling; the Ashkenazic Jews could use gesture: 'And when we buy some food from an Arab in the market, he gesticulates with the fingers. We answer in like manner by hinting to him . . .' (Semyatitsher 1716). Gesture continues to be the typical solution to linguistic insufficiency, and the following transaction, observed in the Old City, is probably a regular occurrence:

Buyer (female, 40, pointing, in Hebrew). *Kamah zeh?* (How much?)
Seller (female villager, 40, showing three fingers, in Arabic). *Tlat miyat, kilo* (300 a kilo).
Buyer (in Hebrew). *Kamah?* (How much?)

Seller (raising hand, adding emphasis and a pause, in Arabic). *Tlat miyat, kilo* (300 a kilo).
Buyer (leaving). Ah.

Observed by MH at 4.15 p.m., 21 June 1984, at the Damascus Gate.

Each participant uses her own language, adding gesture to make sure that the statement is understood; the lack of a common language does not seem to block understanding, and necessary conditions 1 and 2 are circumnavigated, as it were, by moving to a shared language of gesture. Clearly, however, such a solution is no more than a temporary expedient: as Mühlhäusler (1988: 44) reminds us, there are major, if unstudied, 'diseconomies arising out of lack of communication channels'.

But there are cases where both interlocutors have more than one language in common: sellers and buyers who each know Arabic, Hebrew, and English. What governs language choice in these cases? More complex rules are called for here, but first we shall turn to another parenthetical issue, that of repeated encounters.

The inertia rule

The purpose of our survey was to explain the choice of language in an initial contact, together with any subsequent changes within the encounter. In practice, many of the language choices observed in such circumstances will have been determined by earlier transactions: when you speak to someone for the second time, you already know what worked the first time you spoke. This general fact is encapsulated in another important rule, governed by the inertia condition:

Language Choice Rule 3 (inertia condition—typical, graded[1]): prefer to use the language[2] of your last encounter with this person.

The inertia condition is a conservative factor in language choice: its obvious economy of effort makes it unlikely that choices, once made, will be changed. To switch the language in which you communicate regularly with someone—a family member, a close friend, a colleague—takes a major effort. Thus, the weight of inertia favours conservatism: it is easier to persuade parents to use a new language when speaking to their young children than it is to persuade them to use it with each other.

But the inertia condition does not apply with a stranger. In initiating a conversation with a stranger in a market-place, the ability to select a suitable language is of obvious importance.

---

[1] This is a typicality condition because it does not always apply; it is a graded condition that becomes stronger the more two people speak to each other.

[2] Or, better, variety or varieties of language. There will be cases where the normal language choice is to use only one language; others where it is to switch between two or more socially determined codes.

Language choices in a bilingual interchange

Topic or domain

The two necessary conditions deal with limitations on language choice, applying absolutely in those circumstances in which one or other of the interlocutors has only one language available, and the other has two. Its translation into an instrumental reason for language learning or teaching is particularly important: if you need to speak to someone who does not know your language, you can either learn that person's language or help that person to learn yours.

If the first two necessary conditions for language choice are met, and the two interlocutors are (or can be expected to be) able to use the same two languages, other conditions are needed to account for choice. The first of these rules relates to the domain. As Fishman (1971) defined it, domain is a construct involving congruence between locale, role-relationship, and topic. Other things being equal, domain contributes to language choice:

Language Choice Rule 4 (domain condition—typical, graded[3]): prefer the language you use most comfortably in the domain of the interchange.

The interesting thing to note about this rule is that it claims not only that an individual's language preference depends on knowing the language and being able to use it, but also that this knowledge and ability is not unitary, that is to say, it may vary from domain to domain depending on personal experience and, at another remove, on the experience (or cultural history) of users of the language as a whole. A similar point is made by Dodson (1985); he maintains that there are no equilinguals, and that even accomplished (or, as he calls them, balanced) bilinguals have a preferred and a second language for various domains and topics. This is clearly a typicality condition; a speaker will often be forced or will consider it appropriate to use a second rather than a preferred language.

The claim for the existence of domain language preference is supported by some of the answers to questions in the Old City study about language use (see Chapter 1). In the course of the first interview, after respondents had answered questions about the language knowledge of members of their household, they were asked to provide information about the frequency with which they themselves used the languages they knew, and the functions for which they used them.[4]

---

[3] It is typical because other conditions may be stronger; it is graded because various topics and domains will have different weightings.

[4] For questions concerning the frequency of use of Hebrew and English, and the functions for which each language was used, this section uses answers given by Muslim or Christian native speakers of Arabic. The total size of this subsample is 299, and its age range, compared to that of the survey population as a whole (the youngest participant in which was 14), is very similar (mean 37 for the subsample, compared to 39 in the survey sample; median 35 compared to 37). Omitting, as it does, all Jewish respondents, the average educational level is lower (8.2 mean, compared to 9.9). There are also more women than men (68 per cent to 32 per cent) in this subsample, something to be

There was a big difference between language knowledge and language use recorded here: quite large proportions of those interviewed reported only rare or occasional use of their other languages. The figures for daily use of another language also showed the importance of English as a second language. It was suggested that, while about a fifth of the native speakers of Arabic claimed to know Hebrew, less than half of that number claimed to use it every day. Similarly, a third claimed to know English, but only half of them to use it daily. However, the fact that half of those who can speak Hebrew and English use the language daily confirms the multilingual nature of the situation; most of us have occasion to use our *foreign* languages only very occasionally; daily use is clearly the mark of a *second*-language situation.

Chapter 1 also gave details of the purposes for which the languages were used. Four main categories of use were reported for Hebrew and English: work, commerce (whether buying or selling), education, and social interaction. For both languages, the most common of these categories was work, a domain in which a fifth of the claims for use of English was found, with a slightly smaller fraction for Hebrew. Even though native speakers of Arabic claimed to be more familiar with English and to use it more often than Hebrew, the closeness of the percentages for use at work for the two languages supports the generalization that Hebrew is mainly a work-language for Arabs. Hebrew was more important for commerce (whether buying or selling) than English was. However, English was used twice as much as Hebrew for social purposes, and was also the dominant language in education.

So, the Arabs in the sample used English more often than Hebrew, but this increased use came from the fact that it served a wider range of purposes: Hebrew was mainly restricted to work and commerce; English served an equal share in these roles, but was also used for social purposes and education.

Corroboration of this differential use is found by looking at the relation between function and frequency. The frequency with which Arab speakers over the age of 14 use Hebrew, and the purposes for which they use it, are shown in Table 7.2. Work and commerce clearly dominate; a sixth of the sample used Hebrew for work, the majority of them daily. A similar breakdown of use of English is contained in Table 7.3. Work was also the dominant domain here, followed by school, commerce, and social interaction in that order. Table 7.4 provides

expected, because this group comprises only those respondents who were at home during the day, which is when most of the interviews took place. As a result, there is a large proportion of housewives (43 per cent, compared to 20 per cent in the general survey); other occupational classes are fairly well represented. The only other large difference is in the proportion of students. It should be noted that the subsample's exclusion of younger children makes more likely the inclusion of those who speak languages other than Arabic; the number of Hebrew and English speakers turns out to be higher in this group than in the survey as a whole. For instance, 31 per cent of this subsample (compared to 18 per cent of the general sample) is reported as being able to carry on an adult conversation in Hebrew, and 53 per cent (compared to 31 per cent in the main survey) as being able to carry on a conversation in English. There are similar differences for the other skills.

TABLE 7.2. *Use of spoken Hebrew by Palestinians over the age of 14*

Function	Rare	Occasional	Monthly	Weekly	Everyday	Total
Work	5	5	3	3	35	51
Commerce	6	3	4	6	25	44
Social	0	1	0	1	11	13
School	1	0	0	4	5	10

TABLE 7.3. *Use of spoken English by Palestinians over the age of 14*

Function	Rare	Occasional	Monthly	Weekly	Everyday	Total
Work	2	5	1	8	48	64
School	1	6	1	3	28	39
Commerce	2	3	2	5	22	34
Social	1	2	2	3	18	26

TABLE 7.4. *Frequency of total use of Hebrew and English correlated with other factors*

	Hebrew		English
Use for work	0.77		0.66
Use for commerce	0.66		0.41
Use socially	0.43		0.37
Use in school	0.32		0.42
Male	0.49		0.41
English frequency	0.38	Hebrew frequency	0.38
Educational level	0.22		0.29
Hebrew-reading frequency	0.49	English-reading frequency	0.75
Hebrew-writing frequency	0.48	English-writing frequency	0.70
Occupational level	0.16		0.05
Religion Christian	0.02		0.26
Literacy in Arabic	0.24		0.37

correlations for the degree to which these various functions account for the level of use of Hebrew and English. Correlations with other related factors are given for comparison. Work constitutes the best explanation for the high level of use of them both, but commercial use is more important for Hebrew, and educational use is more important for English. The inclusion of the other factors permits some further trends to be noted. It will be seen first that there is more of a correlation between speaking English and reading and writing it than there is with Hebrew. There are no significant differences in level of use of Hebrew between Christians and Muslims, but there is a significant difference between the two groups' use of English: Christians use English more often than Muslims do. Occupation maybe makes a very slight difference with Hebrew, but not with English. Literacy in Arabic is more closely correlated to the level of use of English than it is to Hebrew (bearing out the educational connection), but both correlations are highly significant.

To sum up what emerged from this analysis: about 15 per cent of the Arab respondents were found to use English daily—at work, in education, for commerce, and for social relations. A smaller proportion, about 7 per cent, had reason to use Hebrew daily; this was mainly accounted for by work and commerce, but for some it was also used for educational activities.

So, there is good evidence to support the existence of domain and topical differentiation in controlling language choice. This is also borne out by other informal observations I have made of Arab traders speaking to each other in Hebrew, a case where the strength of the domain rule seems to have overcome the more usually applied necessary conditions.

Accommodation

The necessary conditions (knowledge and communication) were classified as graded conditions in order to allow for those cases where language choice compensates for linguistic weakness on the part of one of the speakers. The domain condition may also be considered to apply differentially, so that once again the weakness of one interlocutor's language control features as a reason for choosing a specific language. There will be cases, however, where each user is (or can be assumed to be) more or less equally at ease in the two languages. The resolution of these cases has to do with the absolute and relative power or status of the two languages concerned; it is partly to be explained by desires for expressing solidarity; and partly by accommodation theory. The rules themselves are simple: the conditions for their weighting are much more complex (see e.g. Breitborde 1983; Genesee 1983). I will start with the notion of accommodation.

Speech accommodation theory was developed in order to account for changes in speech style in the course of conversations: it deals directly, then, with the issue of intraspeaker variation. A recent summary by Beebe and Giles (1984, based largely on Street and Giles 1982) expresses the theory in a few basic propositions. Given the ability and the appropriate social circumstances, people attempt to converge towards the speech pattern of their interlocutors when they desire approval or communicative efficiency. How closely they converge will depend on personal skills and the importance of the need for approval or efficiency. On the other hand, individuals will adhere to their own speech patterns or even diverge from their interlocutors' when they wish either to maintain their own group identity or to dissociate themselves from the interlocutor or to modify his or her speech. Once again, how far they will diverge will depend on personal skills and feelings.

Cooper and Greenbaum (1987) set out to systematize the interactionist model proposed by Freed (1981) and Snow *et al.* (1981) within what they called an 'accommodation' model, using this term somewhat differently, they said, from the way in which Giles does. Their use is broader:

We define accommodation as the adjustment of speech in response to the mutuality which speakers perceive between themselves and their hearers. We suggest that there are four types of mutuality which are relevant: 1) verbal repertoire, 2) background knowledge, 3) solidarity or intimacy, and 4) power. Phenomenologically, these domains correspond to perceptions of knowing (verbal repertoire and background knowledge), feeling (solidarity or intimacy) and doing (power) (Cooper and Greenbaum 1987: MS.)

The issue of a shared verbal repertoire has been dealt with by the first two conditions; but why a bilingual or multilingual speaker chooses to use the (presumedly) bilingual interlocutor's preferred or stronger language rather than his or her own remains to be answered. Following Giles, the speaker will accommodate (converge) or not (diverge) according to the working of a number of complex conditions: desire for social approval, desire for communicative efficiency, desire to assert group identity in an intergroup transaction, desire to dissociate oneself from the interlocutor, desire to change the interlocutor's speech behaviour (to force a change); all of these will be constrained by social norms and by individual and social notions of optimal social distance. Following Cooper and Greenbaum (1987), these factors can be grouped more succinctly under the power and solidarity headings that have been found to cover so much of social behaviour.

We will now state this as an accommodation rule, suggesting the criteria that determine its direction and strength:

Language Choice Rule 5 (accommodation condition—typical, graded): prefer to use what you assume to be the interlocutor's preferred language or some other language (your own or one you value) according to your perception of the transaction and the power or solidarity involved.

Assume that both you and the person to whom you are speaking are equally bilingual; that you are addressing a person you have not spoken to before; that there is no third party involved; and that the conversation takes place in a society with at least two groups of uneven power, each with its associated language. If the interaction is between members of both dominating and dominated groups, the accommodation condition suggests that the convenience of the former will be served by using his or her language, unless he or she chooses to accommodate to the other party. Assume, however, that the conversation is between two members of the dominated group: in such a case, the use of the language of the dominant group will have nothing to do with convenience, but will count as a claim to membership of that group and so to an advantageous status in the current situation. The working of conditions like these depends on the ideological values of both people involved, and derives from general social values.

The power of a language comes from the group who uses, or who proclaims to use, it. In a commercial transaction, it is the buyer who is generally assumed to have this power, the result of his ability to decide where to make his purchases. It is this factor that constrains the seller to use, or if necessary to learn, the language of the buyers. In the nineteenth century the Sephardic Jewish merchants knew, and the Ashkenazic merchants needed to learn, Arabic; under Israeli rule the Arabic-speaking merchants are constrained to use, and so to learn, Hebrew for transactions with Israelis, and English (and other languages) for transactions with tourists.

The solidarity dimension also involves recognition of group identity. My use of my own identifying language (the signs on buildings in languages that could be read by few, if any, passers-by, for instance) asserts my identity. Addressed in English by an Arab official, a young Arab woman in the post office replied immediately in Arabic, firmly cutting off any attempt at the intimacy he might have been tempted to try with a European woman. My use of my interlocutor's identifying language both cancels any claim to power associated with my language and constitutes a possible step towards intimacy. My use of a third language, clearly understood as such, is an effort at neutrality. In transactions with local Arab merchants, for instance, I have frequently found it appropriate to make the initial greeting in Arabic (cancelling the power claim of Hebrew), and then to continue (because of poor control of Arabic) in English, the neutral choice; after a moment, the shopkeepers move into Hebrew, recognizing the dominant rules of the situation.

The preference in market transactions, however, continues to be for multi-lingualism, as the following trilingual exchange demonstrates:

Four women soldiers walk up to look at bracelets outside a jewellery shop in the market-place.
1. *Shopkeeper 1* (in English). You want bracelets?
2. *Soldier 1* (in English). How much?
3. *Shopkeeper 1* (pointing, in English). You want this one or this one?
4. *Soldier 2* (in Hebrew). *Eleh lo yaffot* (Those aren't pretty).
5. *Soldier 1* (in Arabic). *Hathi, mish xilu?* (That's not pretty?)
6. *Shopkeeper 1* (in Arabic, not transcribed).
7. *Shopkeeper 2* (laughing, in Arabic). *Xilu* (Pretty), (in Hebrew) *Kmo xayalot* (Like women soldiers).

Observed by MH at 4.30 p.m., 5 July 1984.

The shopkeeper starts his business in English (1), in spite of the fact that the soldiers are obviously native speakers of Hebrew. This breach of what we postulated earlier as the seller's condition must be assumed to have some strong significance; it cannot simply be a matter of the shopkeeper's inability to speak

Hebrew. We must conclude, then, that it relates to what was referred to earlier as the symbolic condition, and what in the present chapter is formulated as the accommodation condition, a condition covering values associated with the languages.

What values are involved? The results of our survey make clear that Hebrew has a higher status than Arabic; however, there is also a claim of national identity involved. For the Arab to use Hebrew would be to confirm his subordinate status. By using English, he is offsetting the nationalist value and claiming the higher status associated with English (the language of education and international exchange); he is, at the least, neutralizing the relationship. The first soldier (2) respects this choice by not switching languages; this is a manifest case of accommodation, and permits the shopkeeper to continue in the neutral language (3). At this point (4) the second soldier uses Hebrew to make a comment to the other soldiers. There are two possible explanations for this: first, the conservative or inertia condition makes it highly improbable that the soldiers would address each other in anything else but Hebrew; and, second, it could also be a bargaining ploy, the assumption being that the shopkeeper will understand. The first soldier now switches to Arabic (5); by going one stage further and accommodating not just to the shopkeeper's neutral language choice but even to his own native language, she is at the same time making clear that she is not an English-speaking tourist nor even the kind of non-Arabic-speaking shopper who can be taken advantage of. The shopkeeper accepts the switch (6). Now comes the finale (7): the second shopkeeper shows off his linguistic skills with a pun using the vernacular Arabic word, *xilu*, 'pretty' or 'nice', in the same sentence as the similar-sounding Hebrew word, *xayalot*, 'women soldiers'. This utterance establishes his own status as a Hebrew speaker and at the same time signals approval of the soldier's willingness to use Arabic, reciprocating the accommodation involved. Each of the languages has been made to serve a purpose, and a friendly atmosphere has been maintained.

Jews will often use Arabic for greetings and social leave-takings, but return to Hebrew for the actual bargaining. One respondent, a 48-year-old Iraqi-born Jew who has been living in Israel since the age of 14, reported to me that he uses Arabic in shops where he is known, but Hebrew in strange shops, 'so as not to be fooled by the shopkeeper'.

This last case introduces us to the existence of tension in the linguistic imbalance. An 18-year-old Arab, educated at the Collège des Frères and working in a souvenir shop, stated that although he had picked up Hebrew in the street, he would rather use Arabic when bargaining with Hebrew speakers. A 70-year-old Arab, who claimed to be a seventh-generation Greek Orthodox Christian and to have picked up Hebrew during the period of the Mandate and in the British army, said that he did not like doing business with Israeli Jews, preferring to use English rather than Hebrew with them. A 45-year-old Jew born in Egypt, resident in Israel for fifteen years after fifteen years in France, who appeared to know Arabic perfectly well (one neighbour thought he was a native speaker, but he claimed that French was his mother tongue), maintained that he did better business when he used Arabic; he therefore used it even with those Arabs who addressed him in Hebrew (including one Arab whom he knew to speak Hebrew at home).

I suspect that, underlying this whole issue, is the fact that the rules of bargaining are more important than the language. Agreement is possible even when the two parties do not share a language. And, conversely, even when they do share a language, disagreement over the rules of social discourse is still a distinct possibility, reminding one of George Bernard Shaw's characterization of England and America as two nations divided by a common language. The phenomenon can be exemplified by the following observed transaction:

Tourist (in English). I'm looking for earrings.
Shopkeeper (in English). Please, choose.
Tourist (in English). How much are they?
Shopkeeper (in English). Take your choice.
Tourist (in English). I want a few.
Shopkeeper (in English). How much, a hundred? Eighty? Fifty?
Tourist (in English). A few . . .
Shopkeeper (to another shopkeeper, in Arabic). 40?
Tourist (in English). Three.
Shopkeeper (to observer, in Hebrew). *Ken adon?* (Yes, sir?)
              Observed by MH, 5 July 1984, inside shop selling trinkets.

The tourist and the shopkeeper have no difficulty with language, having chosen to use English, a language with which they are both familiar. The tourist asks for the price too soon, however, and then wants to bargain by offering to make a quantity purchase. The shopkeeper does not take this seriously, turning away first to another person working with him in the shop, and then to another potential customer.

A clue to what was going on here was provided by one of our respondents, an 18-year-old Arab working in a souvenir shop, who said that if a person entering the shop did not greet him in Arabic, as an Arab would, he would always start the conversation in English. On the discourse level, the formal structure for an acceptable Arab bargaining transaction goes something like this:

1. Greetings, establishment of social interaction.
2. Clarification by the buyer of what he intends to buy.
3. Establishment by the seller of its value to him.
4. Bargaining.
5. Decision on price (often with concurrence of bystander).
6. Sale.
7. Leave-taking.

To ask the price directly clearly lowers the value of the whole transaction; to ask it before the buyer has communicated (however delicately and indirectly) his intentions is not acceptable behaviour.

The structure is actually more complex than I have implied so far. The bargaining itself may be long and complex, ideally involving a third party. I was introduced to this concept in practice some years ago, when I accompanied my wife on an expedition to buy some hassocks in the Old City. She had purchased some a few days before, and was returning with me to the same shop. First, the shopkeeper offered us a seat and ordered some soft drinks. My wife explained that she wanted to buy another three hassocks, and I made clear that she was doing the buying; I was just a bystander. The shopkeeper later took advantage of this fact when, having suggested a price, he leaned over to me and whispered: 'Say it is too much.' My role as a bystander would later be to support the seller when an acceptable price had been reached.

Bargaining is a complex business, and each culture has its own rules. The wise buyer appreciates the flexibility in the situation, and takes advantage of it; thus, shrewd consumers in the United States will decide to buy a car at the end of the month from a salesman who is close to a sales record that will bring him or his firm a bonus. But the absence of common rules, and, even worse, the conflict between systems, can lead to serious discomfort.

Caplan (1980) devotes a chapter to bargaining in the Old City market-place, analyzing why it is that many transactions between Arab shopkeepers and Ashkenazic Israelis or tourists 'often ended in mutual frustration and anger' (1980: 82). There are, he suggests, two distinct traditions of bargaining. The European tradition views the market-place as a battlefield, with the seller praising his wares and the buyer attempting to show that they are not worth the price. The European bargainer considers it normal and appropriate behaviour to point out defects in the objects, but many Westerners, Caplan suggests, do not like to use this technique to take advantage of seemingly poor shopkeepers. Arab shopkeepers, for their part, are in fact made uncomfortable by this sharp and insulting style, and either set high prices or make it clear that they prefer not to deal with Israelis.

The Oriental style, Caplan suggests, is quite different; bargaining is seen as an enjoyable pastime, one in which both sides can take pleasure. As it is a social relationship, the shopkeeper feels most comfortable with customers he knows. Regular customers need not bargain; many men confirmed that they often paid the asking price, but women were reported as being more willing to bargain. One shopkeeper told Caplan that he usually asked 25 per cent above the wholesale price from regular customers, whom he assumed would pay without bargaining, but 40 per cent above cost from strangers, who could be expected to bargain.

Caplan also describes some of the techniques he observed during bargaining transactions. The seller's initial price was assumed to be about 25 per cent above value; the customer would offer 50 per cent of the asking price, and then agree to the compromise. The customer's first offer was considered (by both parties) as a joke. Acceptable arguments for offering a lower price included the availability of goods elsewhere at that price, or the temporary limitation of funds available to the customer. In neither circumstance did the customer abuse the goods (or the seller); his offer of a lower price was usually combined with praise for both. Given the conflict between the two styles, it is immediately apparent how a common language could easily turn out to be a source of misunderstanding and friction.

The third-party condition

So far we have been dealing with rules to be applied to the two interlocutors in a transaction. But there can often be a third person present, with an effect on language choice which is captured in the third-party condition:

> Language Choice Rule 6 (third-party condition—typical): prefer to use a language that includes or excludes a third party.

There are situations in which it is deemed important for a third party to be able to understand what is going on; similarly, there are circumstances to which the opposite pertains, or in which this condition has no weight at all. In the second conversation quoted earlier (p. 110), the switch to Arabic and then to Hebrew effectively cut off the unsatisfactory exchange with the tourist. However, in the jewellery shop transaction (p. 108), the first soldier's switch to Hebrew served to strengthen the shopkeeper's disapproval; it was the second soldier's immediate switch to Arabic that restored the friendliness of the exchange, capped by the second shopkeeper's jocular comment in Hebrew.

In conclusion, then, the model I am proposing for language choice is a competence model: a set of rules underlying the understanding of a competent member of a speech community. In Noam Chomsky's attempt to explain linguistic competence this person was an idealized monolingual; in a socio-linguistic description it is of necessity someone who shares not just the community's rules for forming sentences (linguistic competence in its narrowest sense), but its rules for language use (communicative competence). However, knowing the rules is not the same as using them; in practice, there will be cases where mistakes are made or where knowledge is imperfect. In describing the rules of a speech community, there is an additional complication, in that various members of the community will have different values and so apply the same rules differently.

These rules describe a given speech community's assumptions about appropriate language choice: they set, in other words, what Genesee and Bourhis (1983) refer to as 'the situational norm'. This sets the expectations against which an actual performance is judged, providing an ordered set of hypotheses to be tested in real life. If someone addresses me in a language with which I am not familiar, my first (and most charitable) conclusions are either that he thinks I do know it or that he cannot speak any other: once I have corrected the first deduction, his persistence is judged to be because of the second; if I later find that this is not so, I then move on to a finer analysis.

But the various conditions themselves obtain their respective weighting in a number of ways. First, there is the question of the relative salience to the situation of the various domains or clusters of role-relationships; is this a situation in which it is appropriate/valuable to assert a particular role-relationship by choosing a certain language? For example, when meeting a student outside class, the foreign-language teacher may choose to stress the teacher role by using the foreign language or the fellow-citizen role by using the native language. (It is under this heading that I would prefer to consider the assertion of group membership.) Second, there is the issue of the status of the language itself, a cluster of attributes which, as we saw earlier in this chapter, arise in part from the functions with which the language is associated and in part from the status of those who are assumed to use the language. Third, there are the specific and immediate functional claims of the situation, analysed by Scotton (1983) in her work on negotiation. For instance, in order to obtain a better price, the customer might choose to use the seller's language, deviating from the usual principle of sellers accommodating to customers.

Another way of thinking about the issue is to consider the pressure of the various rules. Assuming the knowledge of the speaker and the interlocutor as given, and assuming each to be bilingual, any one of three primary motivations can be of maximum salience: the economic (one speaker's desire to benefit economically from the other), the political (one speaker's desire to assert political dominance, or to recognize the other's political dominance), and the socio-cultural (one speaker's desire to claim social or cultural identity through language use). Becoming an effective communicator in the market-places of the Old City means not just being able to speak several of the languages of the place, but also being able to shift from one to another in the appropriate circumstances in order to find the correct balance between these forces.

8

Reflections of Language Planning

INTERGROUP conflict over scarce resources leads to the use of whatever ammunition lies at hand. Language is a potentially powerful missile, and language planning is the weapon through which that missile is fired. Language planning refers to deliberate efforts to influence the language behaviour of others. The promotion of Hebrew as an all-purpose vernacular in late nineteenth-century and early twentieth-century Palestine is a notable example. Other well-known instances include efforts to cleanse modern Turkish of Arabic and Persian loanwords, the successive switches from Arabic to Latin to Cyrillic script for writing Turkic languages in Soviet Central Asia, the feminist campaign against sex-bias in language usage, the Arabicization movement in North Africa and the Sudan, and the American bilingual-education movement.

A widespread and long-standing practice, language planning is typically motivated by the desire to secure or maintain interests. The promotion of Hebrew, for example, served to mobilize support for political self-determination. The Jewish settlers' use of their ancestors' language in its native land symbolized the continuity of Jewish attachment to that land, an attachment which legitimized attempts to re-establish a national home there. Further, the new settlers' use of Hebrew distinguished them from the traditional, 'old-fashioned' Palestinian Jews, who avoided using Hebrew for secular purposes, a distinction which helped to validate their claims to leadership of the Jewish community in Palestine.

Inasmuch as the Old City of Jerusalem is a spectacular arena for the collision of interests—with Arab and Jew, Palestinian and Israeli, Christian and Muslim, and tourist and local interacting with one another—one can expect to see language planning reflected within its walls. In this chapter some of the results of the socio-linguistic survey and the survey of signs will be examined through the lens provided by language planning.

Students of language planning generally follow Kloss (1969) in distinguishing two focuses for language planning: status planning and corpus planning. Status planning is the attempt to regulate, influence, or determine the language or language variety to be used for given purposes within particular settings. Corpus planning is the attempt to influence spoken or written forms—activities such as coining new terms, reforming spelling, adopting a new script, and making decisions about competing forms when it comes to standardization. I would like to propose a third focus for language planning, namely, acquisition planning, which is directed towards an increase in the number of users of a language—speakers, writers, listeners, or readers (Cooper 1987).

Status planning

When the British captured Palestine from the Ottoman Turks in 1918, they found a large Jewish minority among the majority Arab population. By that time Hebrew had become the principal language of public interaction among the Jewish population. There was, of course, no rival to Arabic as the language, both public and private, of the Arab population. When the British accepted a mandate from the League of Nations in 1922 to administer Palestine, they declared English, Arabic, and Hebrew (in that order) to be the official languages of the territory. Trilingual street signs like the one on the Jaffa Gate (see Fig. 1.5), with English first, Arabic next, and Hebrew last, date from this Mandate period. When Israel emerged as a sovereign state in 1948, all laws in effect under the British remained in force until specifically repealed or amended. The language law was one of the first to be modified. In 1948 the legal requirement to use English was repealed, thus leaving Arabic and Hebrew as the official languages.

Although the official status of English is no longer fixed by law, it continues to be used for many government functions. For example, paper currency, metal coins, and postage stamps are trilingual in Arabic, English, and Hebrew. The street signs put up by the Israelis in the Old City after 1967 are, like the Mandate signs, trilingual, except that now the order is reversed, with Hebrew on top and English on the bottom (see Fig. 1.3). Even during the Jordanian occupation of the Old City English continued to appear on new street signs, although Hebrew was not used (see Fig. 1.4).

Why are languages declared to be 'official'? Certainly, such declarations are unnecessary for any immediate practical purpose. Many countries, including the United Kingdom and the United States, have no statute specifying an official language. Conversely, statutory official languages are sometimes ignored. In Tunisia, for example, where Arabic is the state language, only two out of sixteen ministries were totally Arabicized—with all documents, reports, and publications in Arabic only—as late as 1984. More than thirty years after independence some Tunisian ministries still used French as the language of record, and others operated more or less bilingually (Daoud 1987).

Since it is necessary neither to specify an official language nor to observe it once specified, we must look to the symbolic uses of a statutory official language rather than to its immediate, practical value. When a community views its language as a symbol of its common memory and aspirations, specification of that language as 'official' serves to support the legitimacy of government authority. When a government recognizes the language of a subordinate minority as official (as Arabic is officially recognized in Israel), this constitutes in effect the symbolic acknowledgement of that group's right to maintain its distinctiveness. Conversely, the defacing of Arabic portions of trilingual signs, occasionally found in the Jewish quarter of the Old City (see Fig. 6.8), represents a denial of the validity of that distinctiveness. In most cases, the specification of statutory official languages is an exercise in the manipulation of political symbols for the maintenance of government authority.

There has never been a special statute specifying the official languages of Jerusalem as distinct from those of the state itself. Indeed, such a ruling would imply a special status for Jerusalem, a state of affairs desired by none of its rulers, who have claimed it as an integral part first of Mandate Palestine, then of the Hashemite Kingdom of Jordan, and finally of the state of Israel. Still, the use of the territory-wide official languages in the Old City has borne considerable symbolic freight. Mandate trilingual signs with English on top declared in effect that the British were rulers of Jerusalem, with its two indigenous national groups. When the Jordanians conquered the Old City, their use of Arabic–English signs, with Arabic on top and then an English transliteration of the Arabic, indicated Jordanian suzerainty—the absence of Hebrew in effect declared the Jewish claims to the Old City to be illegitimate; indeed, all Jewish residents were forced to leave the Old City, and Jews were denied access to their holy places. When the Israelis captured the Old City in 1967, thereby restoring the millennia-long Jewish presence there, the use of trilingual signs—this time with Hebrew on top and English as a transliteration of the Hebrew—indicated, even before the formal annexation of the Old City some years later, that the Jews were in charge but that they recognized the Arab presence and its right to self-definition. For the Jewish minority in the Old City, surrounded by a hostile population and by archaeological reminders not only of past glories but also of past humiliations, the street signs serve as a reminder, a reassurance, that the state defends their presence. For the Arab majority, in daily contact with Israeli policemen, the street signs serve as yet another reminder that they are once again subordinate to an alien power.

An even more humiliating reminder of subjugation for the Arab majority are two new signs at the front of the Kishleh, the massive police barracks built by the Turks near the Jaffa Gate. A few years ago there was a small trilingual sign above its arched entrance (see Fig. 8.1), but this was replaced for a while by one of the largest signs in the Old City, which had 'POLICE' written on it in two languages, Hebrew and English, and the starred insignia of the police force between the two. A similar but smaller sign (see Fig. 8.2) rests on a post to the left of the entrance. Indeed, similar bilingual signs identify all police stations, police vehicles, and police barricades throughout Israel and the administered territories. For whatever reason, the large sign was taken down towards the end of 1989.

The signs at the front of the Kishleh do more than identify it, however; in fact, no resident of the Old City needs to be told its location. Just as the signs on police vehicles, call-boxes, and barricades identify those items as the property of the police, so the Hebrew–English bilingual signs identify the police, symbol and agent of the state's coercive power, as the property of the Jews. The use of these bilingual police signs, on which one of the languages is *not* an official language, is

FIG. 8.1. *Trilingual police sign*

FIG. 8.2. *Bilingual police sign*

doubly insulting: there is room for two languages, but there is no room for Arabic. (Perhaps one could claim that, at the Kishleh at any rate, the English on these police signs is meant for foreign visitors, but that claim is weakened by the presence of a smaller sign in English only, which reads 'TOURIST POLICE'.) To Arab residents of the Old City the bilingual police signs give a clear message: the Old City, in which you are a majority, is not under your control; this police station, staffed primarily by Arab policemen, is not your police station; this state is not your state.

An interesting balance to this case is provided by another linguistic modification to a sign, this time to a 'BANK LEUMI' branch-office sign opposite the Kishleh. For many years the sign used here was a nationally standardized one, in Hebrew and English only, in spite of the fact that a large proportion of the customers of the branch are Arab shopkeepers or Arab residents collecting Israeli social security payments, and that the manager and most of the officials in the branch are themselves Arabs. Just before the police station changed to its bilingual signs, omitting Arabic, the bank put up a new, specially made sign, trilingual in Hebrew, Arabic, and English. This trilingual sign (see Fig. 8.3) may be contrasted with the earlier bilingual sign in Hebrew and English (see Fig. 8.4).

A third case of changes in official language policy may be found in the signs on the post office near the Jaffa Gate. Until a year or so ago, the sign here was bilingual, in Hebrew and French, the latter language recognizing a tie with the

FIG. 8.3. *Trilingual bank sign*

FIG. 8.4. *Bilingual bank sign*

International Postal Union and also echoing an early post-independence spirit of Anglophobia (see Fig. 8.5). Post offices throughout the country have had a new look recently: the signs are now red rather than blue, and the three languages used are Hebrew, Arabic, and English (see Fig. 8.6).

If the specification of a state's official languages is of largely symbolic significance, the language policy of a country's schools is of enormous practical significance. The language policy of Israeli public schools will be unintelligible to the reader who does not know that Arab and Jewish children study in different schools. This segregation, in place long before the founding of the state, is a matter of custom rather than law. No statute forbids mixed schools; indeed, there are a few Arab children in Jewish schools. To the majority of Jewish and Arab citizens, however, a mixed Arab–Jewish school system would be no more conceivable than a single system within each community. As we have already mentioned, Jewish schools are divided into secular and religious, with the latter being subdivided further into state religious, independent religious, and a large number of sectarian religious schools; a proposal to split the state religious schools into two sections, the second of which will be labelled something like state Zionist religious-independent, is currently being debated. The Arab system, too, is divided into state, Muslim, and various sectarian Christian schools.

FIG. 8.5. *Bilingual post office sign*

FIG. 8.6. *Trilingual post office sign*

There are two languages of instruction in this multiple school system: Arabic in the Arab schools, and Hebrew in the Jewish schools. Again, this state of affairs is taken for granted by the public. I once asked my students in a university seminar whether they thought parents would be willing to send their children to an English-medium school. They all agreed that such a school would find a ready market, in both the Arab and the Jewish sectors, given parents' desire for their children to learn English well. I then asked whether Arab parents might be willing to send their children to Hebrew-medium Arab schools, and whether Jewish parents might be willing to send their children to Arabic-medium Jewish schools, in order to promote their children's acquisition of the other group's language. Both the Arab and the Jewish students in my seminar were deeply shocked: 'Oh, Professor Cooper,' one of my students replied slowly, in the tone of voice one might employ towards a dim-witted person, 'English is a neutral language in Israel, but not Arabic or Hebrew!' Thus, each group studies via its own language, at least at the elementary-school level. Some Arab students in state schools study Jewish subjects like the Bible in Hebrew. A group of parents in Tel Aviv are attempting to establish an Arab–Jewish school, and encountering the predictable difficulties. Another symmetry lies in the requirement that each group, Arab and Jewish, study English as a foreign language, but here, with this language requirement, the symmetry ends. Whereas the study of Hebrew as a second language is mandatory for all Arab pupils in state schools in Israel (and therefore in the Arab state schools in Jerusalem, where Israeli law applies), the teaching of Arabic in Jewish state schools is somewhat limited. Spoken Arabic is supposed to be a compulsory subject for Jewish students in the fourth, fifth and sixth grades of elementary school, but the policy is not implemented in many schools (Ben-Rafael and Brosh 1989). Literary Arabic is an optional subject in some high schools.

The first change of language policy in schools in the Old City came in 1962, when Jordanian law required that all schools, private as well as public, begin to use Arabic as the language of instruction, reversing a long-established practice of using metropolitan European languages in the private, Church-supported schools. After Israel captured East Jerusalem in 1967, many Arab parents withdrew their children from the public schools, which came under the supervision of the Israeli Ministry of Education, and enrolled them in private schools. In the Old City, in fact, most of the Arab schools are private schools: no Hebrew is taught here. Similarly, Ministry policy is not implemented in the Old City Jewish schools, and no Arabic is taught here. Thus, in the Old City, where Arabs and Jews are in such close physical proximity, each community seems to be trying to deny the legitimacy of the other's presence by, among other things, refusing to teach the other's language. In contrast, the Old City Armenian school teaches both Arabic and Hebrew as second languages (Hany 1983), an example of the greater pragmatism of a real minority.

As we have seen, most of those Arab residents of the Old City who have managed to learn Hebrew have done so by informal means, a state of affairs promoted, in part, by the language policy of the Old City schools. That few Old City Jews have learned Arabic has probably resulted less from the Old City Jewish schools' neglect of Arabic than from the absence of any material incentives to learn it.

Corpus planning

Corpus planning refers to deliberate efforts to influence spoken or written language forms. Implementation of status-planning decisions frequently demands corpus planning, particularly when a language or language variety is chosen to fulfil a new communicative function. For example, when late nineteenth- and early twentieth-century Palestinian Jews started to use Hebrew as a medium of instruction in the schools of the *yishuv*, they had either to find or to create the terminology to discuss modern school subjects. Accordingly, in 1904 the teachers' union revived the Hebrew Language Council, which had collapsed a few months after its foundation in 1890, to serve the needs of the school system. The Council devoted a great deal of attention to devising school and curriculum terminologies, and after fifty years these had been established for almost all school subjects through high school (Fellman 1977; Rubin 1977).

Confronted with the need for everyday Hebrew vocabulary, the Hebrew Language Council decided initially to use ancient Hebrew words, turning to ancient Aramaic as a back-up when necessary. (Over the centuries, Aramaic had become almost as sacred a Jewish language as Hebrew, which came to be written in the Aramaic alphabet.) If neither Hebrew nor Aramaic words could be found, the Council decided that other Semitic languages would be used as a source; words from non-Semitic languages were initially thought unsuitable. If terms had to be created *de novo*, then Hebrew roots were to be used; failing these, the roots from other Semitic languages, particularly those of Arabic, provided an acceptable alternative (Fainberg 1983). The use of Hebrew and Aramaic sources emphasized the antiquity of the Jewish presence in Palestine, helping to legitimize Jewish claims for self-determination in the land of their Hebrew-speaking ancestors. It is interesting to note that, at the beginning of the century, these nationalists saw other Semitic sources, including Arabic, as consistent with the promotion of the Jewish national movement.

Not all corpus planning, however, arises as a consequence of a language serving a new function. For example, when Israeli Jewish activists began to promote the substitution of the biblical terms 'Judaea' and 'Samaria' for what the Jordanians, to mark their 1948 occupation and the changing of the name of their country from Transjordan, started to call 'the West Bank', they did so to encourage acceptance of their view that these territories constitute an inalienable part of the land of Israel. These activists were not promoting the use of Hebrew for new functions. In much the same way, the recent tendency to restrict the term 'Palestinian' to Palestinian Arabs and its new nationalistic associations may be seen as a case of corpus planning.

Whether or not corpus planning follows the use of a language for new functions, non-communicative goals influence the desired form of the corpus. Where Hebrew at the turn of the century is concerned, we see corpus planning in the service of political goals.

Corpus planning continues on behalf of modern Hebrew, particularly with respect to the standardization of spelling (Rabin 1973) and the modernization of terminology (Fellman and Fishman 1977). In contrast, there is no corpus planning on behalf of a Palestinian Arabic, no effort to magnify, emphasize, or create differences between Palestinian Arabic and the Arabic of other parts of the Arab world in an effort to legitimize claims for Palestinian Arab independence, except for the way in which socio-linguists refer to the local variety as 'Palestinian Arabic'. The most plausible reason for this is that Palestinians seek independence not from another Arab state which claims Palestine as part of its patrimony and from which a separate identity must be forged and maintained, but rather from a Hebrew-speaking Israel from which Palestinians are clearly separate.

Another reason is the Arabs' veneration of literary Arabic. Regarding this elevated, written variety as their real language, Arabs view the grammatically and lexically distinct 'low' variety, the vernacular used in everyday discourse, as scarcely a language at all (Ferguson 1959). Inasmuch as the Palestinian vernacular would be the grounds for forging a distinctive Palestinian Arabic, it is not surprising that, as yet, no efforts have been mounted in that direction.

Acquisition planning

Acquisition planning refers to organized efforts to promote language learning by creating or enhancing opportunities or incentives to learn. The major examples offered by our socio-linguistic survey are: (1) the learning of literary Arabic by Arabic mother-tongue speakers; (2) the learning of Hebrew as a second language by Arabic mother-tongue speakers; (3) the learning of Hebrew as a second language by Jewish immigrants to Israel; and (4) the learning of English as a foreign language by all ethnolinguistic groups. In all these cases we can see organized efforts to create or improve either the opportunity to learn, or the incentive to learn, the target language.

With respect to the learning of literary Arabic and English, this opportunity is created primarily via formal class-room instruction, from primary school through university. In addition, night-school courses in English are offered to adults by such agencies as the British Council, the YMCA, the Martin Buber Centre of the Hebrew University, the Open University, and the Jerusalem municipality.

There are strong economic incentives for Arabic mother-tongue speakers to learn to read and write Arabic, and for all ethnolinguistic groups to learn English. None the less, these incentives are strengthened by setting English as a compulsory subject on the Israeli matriculation examination, and English and Arabic as compulsory subjects on the Jordanian matriculation examination. Most of the Arabic mother-tongue speakers in the Old City who sit for a matriculation examination take the Jordanian rather than the Israeli examination. To the extent that university entrance and the first stages of many jobs require a matriculation certificate, the incentive to learn literary Arabic and English is increased by setting those subjects as compulsory for matriculation.

The promotion of Hebrew among new immigrants is conducted through a variety of means. For many years, 'absorption centres', where immigrants live while sorting out their employment and housing arrangements, have offered subsidized, on-site, intensive six-month Hebrew classes. Other classes, intensive and non-intensive, are offered by municipalities for nominal fees. Universities offer special courses for foreign students and for immigrant lecturers and their spouses. When immigrant children go to school, they are offered instruction in Hebrew as a second language if there are enough children to form a class. Otherwise, children may be pulled out of their classes for a few hours of individual instruction per week. A weekly newspaper is published in simplified Hebrew, and Hebrew literature is published in simplified Hebrew. A television series in simplified Hebrew, produced in the 1970s, is rebroadcast from time to time. Finally, the news is broadcast twice a day in simplified and slower Hebrew.

As for creating incentives to learn, Hebrew is a required subject on the Israeli matriculation examination, but this affects relatively few immigrants, most of whom arrive as adults, and relatively few Arabs in the Old City. As indicated above, most Old City Arabs refuse to take the Israeli matriculation examination. For most Jewish immigrants, the reasons for learning Hebrew are valid enough not to require the imposition of additional incentives. In fact, given the tremendous incentives and learning opportunities of everyday life, it is difficult to determine the extent of the impact of planned procedures on immigrants' acquisition of Hebrew. Once Hebrew became the principal language of Jewish public life in Palestine, the likelihood was that newcomers would learn it with or without organized efforts to help them do so. Indeed, Schmelz and Bachi (1974: 769) suggest that the number of adult immigrants who have learned Hebrew exceeds any reasonable estimate of the direct output, quantitatively or qualitatively, of formal instruction.

What efforts are made to teach Hebrew to Arab children? As stated above, all Arab children in Israeli public schools must study Hebrew from elementary school onwards, and Hebrew is a compulsory subject on the Israeli matriculation examination for both Arab and Jewish students. Those children attending Arab public schools in East Jerusalem must also study Hebrew. Further, publicly supported Hebrew courses, other than those offered by the absorption centres, are open to Arabs as well as to Jews, although the former constitute a small proportion of the students. Moreover, the simplified Hebrew newspaper and books and the simplified Hebrew radio and television programmes are available to Arab as well as to Jewish students.

In comparison to these efforts to teach Hebrew to the Arab population, efforts to spread Arabic among the Jewish population are less impressive. Why is Arabic not a compulsory subject of instruction for Jewish high-school as well as elementary-school children? Why is Arabic not a compulsory subject for the Israeli matriculation certificate? The most plausible explanation is that the Jewish public sees little practical use in learning Arabic: 'Let the Arabs learn Hebrew', as some of our respondents said, seems to be the dominant Jewish view. Indeed, Arabs do learn Hebrew, even when the opportunities for formal instruction are relatively meagre, as our socio-linguistic survey has shown. There have been some attempts to remedy this lack of knowledge of Arabic, however. In 1989 the Minister of Education called for Arabic to be taught in all Israeli Jewish schools, echoing a position taken by the Education Committee of the Knesset in 1976 (Ben-Rafael and Brosh 1989). The army is currently involved in training teachers: programmes are provided at teachers' colleges and universities, and a number of Israelis perform their army service by teaching Arabic in Jewish schools.

To summarize: language planning in Israel, as reflected in the Old City of Jerusalem, seems to have been directed chiefly towards the legitimization and maintenance of Jewish hegemony over Palestine/Israel, the spread of Hebrew as a second language among the Arab population, and the gathering and assimilation of Jewish immigrants. Palestinian language planning, as reflected in the Old City, seems to be directed towards the rejection of Israeli suzerainty rather than towards the legitimization and strengthening of Palestinian claims to autonomy.

9

Language Learning

THE Old City is manifestly multilingual. As Chapter 1 has shown, close to half of the population in our sample, of whatever age, was reported to know at least one other language besides a mother tongue, a fifth of the total was said to know two other languages, and a quarter was claimed to know three or more languages. The task of this chapter is to help to account for that knowledge by showing how these languages were learned.

Monolinguals, bilinguals, and multilinguals

A language may be acquired as a mother tongue—that is, learned by itself or with another language during the first two or three years of life from parents or other caretakers—or learned subsequently, either formally or informally. It was mother-tongue learning that accounted for the overall pattern in the Old City, and that explained why the Muslim and Christian communities as a whole were Arabic speaking. This was made clear in the second survey: all but two of the Muslim or Christian Arabs in this small sample said that they were native speakers of Arabic. Mother-tongue learning also accounted for the main language of the Armenian community (a change, as Chapter 2 stated, from the nineteenth-century situation, when the Armenians spoke Arabic as their first language) and for the home languages of the much smaller communities. These minor languages were learned by non-native speakers as a result of intermarriage only: either you are a mother-tongue speaker of such a language yourself, or you learn it when you marry a mother-tongue speaker. Although it is discouraged, Turkish continues to be spoken in the Armenian quarter by older people, who are also reported to listen to the Turkish radio programmes; many younger people have learned it from their parents or through contact with Armenian students from Turkey (Azarya 1984: 101–2).

Mother-tongue learning does not define the Hebrew-speaking community; just under half the Jews in the sample over the age of 5 was reported to be native speakers of Hebrew (compared to the finding that 97 per cent of the Muslims and Christians over 5 were native speakers of Arabic, and all of the Armenians were reported to be native speakers of Armenian). However, the vitality of Hebrew as the language of Israeli Jews was substantiated by the fact that 80 per cent of Jews under the age of 5 were said to be native speakers.

Thus, we found Arabic to be the mother tongue of almost all the Arabs, and

Hebrew the mother tongue of almost half of the Jews. As far as the other half was concerned, Hebrew had been learned as a second language either at school, or in special courses, or informally. Mother-tongue learning, however, accounted for only a tiny fraction of English speakers, nor was English known by very young children. English was mainly a second language. With the exception of three Jews and two Arabs in the sample who were native speakers of English, most Jews (75 per cent) and Arabs (69 per cent) had learned their English at school. For 22 per cent of the Jews and 11 per cent of the Arabs, this school instruction had been supplemented by other language courses. Among the Jews in the sample, 31 per cent had lived in an English-speaking environment for at least a month; this was true of only 4 per cent of the Arabs. Arabs claimed to learn or to keep up their English at work (35 per cent) or on the street with tourists (26 per cent); Jews reported this much less (11 per cent at work, 6 per cent on the street). Private study was relatively unimportant (8 per cent among Jews and 4 per cent among Arabs), and the media was not acknowledged as a learning method.

Two mother tongues

It is possible to be a native speaker of more than one language, to learn a second (or third) language at the same time and in the same place as the first. Some interesting trends emerge as a result of studying the thirty-one people in the survey for whom this was the case, who were reported to have grown up with more than one mother tongue. These data are summarized in Table 9.1. Five or six of them were the children of immigrants, and were brought up speaking both the immigrant and the new language; ten were children of mixed marriages, where the parents each spoke a different language; eleven grew up in minority communities in the Old City (six Armenian, four Aramaic, and one 'Sudanese');

TABLE 9.1. *Data on bilingualism*

Case	Languages	Religion	Age	Sex	Place of birth	Explanation of bilingualism
1	Arabic/Aramaic	C	60	f	Old City	Mother of no. 11
2	Arabic/Aramaic	C	23	f	Old City	(Father's language is Turkish; 29-year-old brother's language is Arabic

continued overleaf]

Case	Languages	Religion	Age	Sex	Place of birth	Explanation of bilingualism
3	Arabic/Aramaic	C	50	m	Old City	
4	Arabic/Aramaic	C	22	f	Kuwait	
5	Arabic/Armenian	C	8	f	Old City	Mother of no. 18; father Arabic
6	Arabic/Armenian	C	6	f	Old City	Same as no. 19
7	Arabic/Armenian	C	1	m	Old City	Same as no. 19
8	Arabic/English	C	76	m	London	Priest
9	Arabic/French	C	28	m	Lebanon	Priest
10	Arabic/French	C	54	f	Bethlehem	
11	Arabic/Greek	C	57	f	Old City	Mother is Greek
12	Arabic/Greek	C	52	f	Old City	
13	Aramaic/Arabic	C	32	f	Old City	
14	Armenian/Arabic	C	41	f	Jaffa	
15	Armenian/English	C	41	f	Old City	Mother is Armenian; father is British
16	Armenian/Turkish	A	66	f	Jordan	
17	Armenian/Turkish	A	42	m	Old City	Son of no. 30
18	Bukharan/Turkish	M	62	f	Bukhara	
19	Bukharan/Turkish/Arabic	M	50	m	Old City	Son of no. 25
20	English/Hebrew	J	19	f	Jerusalem	US parents
21	French/Hebrew	J	23	f	Petah Tikvah	
22	French/Spanish	J	33	f	Morocco	
23	German/Hebrew	J	46	f	Tel Aviv	
24	German/Hebrew	J	37	m	Jerusalem	
25	Hebrew/French	J	25	f	Jerusalem	
26	Hebrew/Yiddish	J	59	f	Jerusalem	
27	Sudanese/Arabic	M	32	f	Old City	
28	Turkish/Aramaic	C	45	f	Lebanon	
29	Turkish/Arabic	M	63	m	Jenin	Father is Arabic; mother is Turkish
30	Vietnamese/French	C	52	f	France	Nun
31	Yiddish/Hebrew	J	34	f	Jerusalem	

Note: Religions have been abbreviated as follows: C = Christian; M = Muslim; J = Jewish; A = Armenian Christian.

three grew up in bilingual Jewish communities. Especially noteworthy was the fact that three-quarters of those who were reported to have two mother tongues were women, suggesting that girls are more likely to keep up both the language of the home (the mother's language?) and the outside language. This argument is supported in particular by case 11, a 23-year-old woman who reported that she had grown up speaking both Arabic and Aramaic; as her father's first language was Turkish, the Aramaic must have come from the mother, but she also reported that her 29-year-old brother grew up speaking Arabic only.

So, mother-tongue learning accounted for the basic pattern. But, in general, the home provided only the fundamental stages of mother-tongue learning; the more specialized knowledge, especially literacy skills, are handed over to formal instruction. In the case of a strongly diglossic language like Arabic, for instance, the acquisition of skill in the classical or standard (H) variety depends almost entirely on schooling.

Acquiring formal language varieties

Evidence of enhanced mother-tongue knowledge, or, in the case of Arabic, the acquisition of a distinctive formal variety, is most easily seen in the survey by looking at claims for mother-tongue reading ability. Nearly 70 per cent of the Arabic population over the age of 5 were reported as being literate in Arabic, but the figures also demonstrate a change in the level of education: while 95 per cent of those between the ages of 15 and 25 were said to be literate, the figure for the next age-group (26 to 35) was lower (88 per cent), and for those over 36 it was even lower still (73 per cent). The percentage for literacy in Arabic follows a similar trend to that for English speaking and for English and Hebrew literacy.

Another way to look at these data is to analyse the correlations between the various kinds of language knowledge and age, as Table 9.2 shows. One notes that the correlations between age-group on the one hand, and Hebrew and Arabic reading and English reading and speaking on the other, are all about the same

TABLE 9.2. *Correlations between language skills of Arabic mother-tongue speakers*

	Age	Speak Hebrew	Read Hebrew	Speak English	Read English	Read Arabic
Age	1.00	0.71	0.62	0.61	0.56	0.58
Speak Hebrew		1.00	0.94	0.85	0.90	0.68
Read Hebrew			1.00	0.78	0.90	0.57
Speak English				1.00	0.96	0.93
Read English					1.00	0.78
Read Arabic						1.00

(between 0.56 and 0.61), while that between age-group and speaking Hebrew is a little higher (0.71).

Mother-tongue enrichment is provided for Arabic, Hebrew, and Armenian speakers in their respective schools. For speakers of minority languages, however, this enrichment must depend on community or religious support, as with the teaching of Aramaic associated with the Syrian Church. It is also worth mentioning the extra classes in English for native speakers in the Jewish elementary schools.

Mother-tongue learning and school-based mother-tongue enrichment set the basis of the pattern of language knowledge in the Old City. Additional language knowledge can be acquired either formally or informally; this will be the focus of the rest of this chapter.

Formal language learning: The sources of language knowledge

We have already noted that the ability to speak Arabic is most likely to have been acquired as a mother tongue, and that, within our sample, Hebrew is more likely to have been learned as a second language, and English and French are mainly second languages. A second language can be learned in school or in one of its natural environments. We will now attempt to distinguish between these two circumstances for each of the main languages studied. We will start by looking at the learning of English and Hebrew by Palestinians, both Muslim and Christian. Claimed knowledge of these languages within these communities is contained in Table 9.3. Several interesting trends emerge from these figures. Looking first at the columns for both Muslim and Christian native speakers of Arabic, it is to be noted that nearly a fifth is reported to be able to speak Hebrew, and just over a third to be able to speak English. Remember that this figure is for the total population of all ages; for those over 5, nearly a third is claimed to know Hebrew,

TABLE 9.3. *Claimed knowledge of Hebrew and English for all Arabic mother-tongue speakers*

	Muslims (1,318)		Christians (421)		Total (1,739)	
	No.	%	No.	%	No.	%
Speak Hebrew	232	18	84	20	316	18
Read Hebrew	57	4	20	5	77	4
Write Hebrew	64	5	21	5	85	5
Speak English	369	28	232	55	601	34
Read English	159	12	152	36	311	18
Write English	256	19	179	42	435	25

and 45 per cent is claimed to know English. This relative position of the two languages holds for all cases: more Arabic speakers are reported to know English than Hebrew. We will need to look for explanations of this fact.

Second, note that the claims for reading and writing are, in all cases, markedly lower than those for speaking. The figure for writing is higher than that for reading, but this is probably due to the wording of the two questions. As we mentioned in Chapter 1, the questionnaire asked about the ability to read an adult newspaper and to write a simple letter, the word 'simple' perhaps leading some to overestimate their competence with regard to the latter skill. The disparity in spoken and literacy skills reflects the differences in formal and informal learning situations; one may expect reading and writing to have been learned only in a formal situation, while speaking might be learned in either or both.

Comparing Muslims and Christians again, it is interesting to note that, while there are only slight differences in the ability to speak, read, and write Hebrew, the margin is very large when it comes to the same skills in English. One observation to be made here is that this does not seem to accord with the fact that Hebrew is taught only in the Muslim pubic schools (Hany 1983); at first glance, this does not seem to affect the overall situation of Hebrew, nor does the fact that the Christians live closest to the Jews (see below). We will also need to explain why it is that Christians have a superior knowledge of English. This does not come directly from the Church (few, if any, of the Arab Christians worship in English), but can be attributed in part to attendance at schools that teach English, and in part to differences in educational level, for the average level of education is higher for Christian Arabs than it is for Muslims.

Schools

For all its smallness, the Old City has in it a total of twenty-four schools (Hany 1983), ten of them Christian, ten Muslim, and four Jewish. Three of the Muslim schools and two of the Jewish schools are state elementary schools. About one third of the children in Christian schools are Muslims. Many of the children in the Old City attend schools outside the walls; there is, for instance, no Jewish high school. Conversely, some of the children attending schools inside the Old City come from outside. None the less, the school language policy will give some idea of the basis underlying the situation we are describing.

The Christian schools were established at various times in the nineteenth and twentieth centuries, primarily for religious reasons but in part to spread the language or culture of the country involved. Four of the Muslim schools were founded during the period of the Britsh Mandate: a vocational boys school and an academic girls school, established by the Islamic Council and a public boys school and a public girls school, established by the government to train potential civil servants. After 1967 five additional Muslim private schools were set up by the Islamic Council to provide for those Arab pupils who withdrew from the public schools as a result of the switch from the Jordanian to the Israeli curriculum and university entrance examination. A public elementary school for Muslim girls was also established after 1967, intended to enable them to study closer to home. The four Jewish schools were all set up after 1967: two state schools (one secular and one religious), and two private religious schools.

Before 1961 the private Christian schools did a lot of their teaching in other languages, some preparing their students in English for the London matriculation examination, or in French for the baccalaureate. Since 1961 all private schools have followed the Jordanian curriculum, which requires all tuition to be in Arabic. There are two exceptions to this: the Collège des Frères has continued to teach a dual programme, in Arabic for the Jordanian examination and in English for the British general certificate of secondary education (GCSE); and the Armenian school did not accept the ruling, maintaining Armenian studies as the main programme, and the British GCSE as a second programme:

The Saint Tarkmanchatz school is the principal transmitter of Armenian culture to the local community's children . . . The language of instruction in schools is Armenian, ensuring its preservation as the principal spoken and written tongue in the community and preventing any slipping towards local languages. In addition to Armenian, the study of English is emphasized to enable pupils to pass British high school matriculation examinations. Arabic and Hebrew are also taught as secondary foreign languages . . . (Azarya 1984: 101).

Thus, the language of instruction is Arabic in the Muslim and Christian schools, Armenian in the Armenian school, and Hebrew in the Jewish schools. Except for some use of English-language texts in scientific subjects in the Armenian school, and of English in the GCSE subjects at the Collège des Frères, the schools are essentially monolingual. There is, however, a good deal of foreign-language teaching. English is taught in most of the schools, for between three and seven hours a week; Arabic, as noted above, is taught as a foreign language for five hours a week in the Armenian school; Hebrew is taught as a foreign language for five hours a week in the Armenian school, and for three hours a week in the Muslim public schools (thus, about 20 per cent of the non-Jewish children in the Old City have school instruction in Hebrew). Other foreign languages are also taught: French, German, Spanish, and Italian are taught in those Christian schools where it is the language of either the founding or the funding body. French is taught in five Christian schools, German in the Martin Luther school, Spanish in Pilar college, and Italian in the Franciscan orphanages.

As Hany (1983) remarks, the most striking feature of school language policy in the Old City is the reluctance of Arab private schools to teach Hebrew and of Jewish schools to teach Arabic. By default, therefore, the common language of education is English.

Education and age

One factor that helps to explain knowledge of a second language is age: for a language not learned at home, the older one is, the more time there has been to learn it, whether at school or in informal situations. Table 9.4 concentrates on the effect of this factor in particular on the language skills of Arabic mother-tongue speakers. It can be seen that there is an increase in English and Hebrew skills up to the 19–25 age-group, followed by a flattening-off or a decline—except for Hebrew speaking, which continues to rise through the age of 35. The percentage for Arabic literacy follows a similar trend to that for English speaking and English and Hebrew literacy. This suggests that, as a factor, age is probably compounded with the effects of two others—formal education and informal contact.

TABLE 9.4. *Age and language skills of Arabic mother-tongue speakers*

Age-groups	Hebrew		English		Arabic
	Speak	Read	Speak	Read	Read
	%	%	%	%	%
0–9	2	0	3	0	5
10–14	7	1	31	7	77
15–18	20	3	59	31	95
19–25	40	15	69	48	94
26–35	45	10	58	34	88
36+	21	5	40	18	73
All ages	23	6	44	23	73
(SAMPLE SIZE	1374	1318	1381	1359	1500)

Table 9.5 moves on to look at how the Hebrew, English, and Arabic skills of those over 16 are affected by the length of time spent in education. We note that Arabic literacy is reported to be achieved during elementary education, with the main learning taking place during the first six years and the finishing touches during the seventh and eighth years. English-speaking ability, on the other hand, grows evenly with education, reaching its peak among those with post-secondary education (96 per cent), at a level close to that of Arabic literacy (99 per cent). English-reading ability follows the same path, but the growth is slow in elementary school, keeping pace with the learning of English speaking only after the beginning of secondary school; at no time does it attain the same level.

The picture for Hebrew is different; the levels attained are very much lower, and the relation to education is not as clear. Hebrew-reading ability does not rise above 20 per cent, but the growth is closely correlated with education. Hebrew-speaking ability increases fairly rapidly during the elementary-school years, but

TABLE 9.5. *Education and language skills of Arabic mother-tongue speakers*

Years of education	Hebrew		English		Arabic
	Speak	Read	Speak	Read	Read
	%	%	%	%	%
Below 5	6	0	6	1	23
5–6	20	3	27	6	83
7–8	26	6	48	13	96
9–10	37	8	67	35	98
11–12	37	12	86	53	100
13+	40	19	96	82	99
All ages	23	6	44	23	73
(SAMPLE SIZE	1374	1318	1381	1359	1500)

this growth rate is not kept up in the secondary-school years: note the way in which English-reading competence quickly overtakes and surpasses it during this period.

To sum up: English-speaking and -reading ability is most clearly explained by education; similarly, the development of Hebrew-reading skills, however limited, is closely associated with education. The low level supports Hany's (1983) findings that very little Hebrew is taught in Arab schools both in and serving the Old City. Competence in Hebrew speaking, however, is not fully explained by education, and we will need to look for an explanation of this in informal-learning situations.

Informal language learning

One source of informal learning might lie in residential proximity to speakers of another language: if Arabs learn Hebrew informally, we would expect their knowledge to increase with their proximity to Hebrew-speaking Jews. Table 9.6 uses data from twenty-two census cells to determine first the percentages of Jews and non-Jews within each cell, and then the percentages for Arabs' use of Hebrew and English, and Jews' use of Arabic. Three cells had sizeable Jewish populations (over 50 per cent), and two had significant proportions of Jews (about 20 per cent). In three out of these five, the percentage of Arabs speaking Hebrew was much higher than average (about 60 per cent); in one it was average; and in one it was well below average. But it should be noted that in each of the cells supporting this high level of Hebrew-speaking Arabs, there was also a high level of use of spoken English.

Another factor to be explored as an explanation of informal learning is occupation. While this does not at first sight distinguish between formal and informal learning (i.e. occupation could be a motive for, or a result of, the formal learning of another language), if we look closely it does in fact yield interesting information. First, there is a clear relationship between a person's occupation and the number of languages he or she knows. As a whole, for example, academics are most likely to be multilingual, while semi-skilled and unskilled workers are most likely to be monolingual. Table 9.7 contains further data on the 'occupational' use of Hebrew by Arabic speakers over the age of 16. Children are least likely to know Hebrew, followed by unemployed adults (excluding students)

TABLE 9.6. *Proximity and informal language learning*

Cell*	Jews %	Non-Jews %	Arabs speaking Hebrew %	Arabs speaking English %	Jews speaking Arabic %
Muslim Quarter					
00	0	100	27	39	—
01	0	100	20	54	—
02	0	100	36	48	—
03	0	100	7	8	—
04	0	100	16	35	—
05	0	100	19	43	—
87	0	100	23	28	—
88	0	100	26	35	—
89	0	100	18	37	—
90	0	100	23	51	—
91	0	100	12	48	—
98	0	100	16	42	—
99	0	100	28	42	—
Armenian Quarter					
06	69	31	66	80	28
92	25	75	28	75	19
93	21	79	60	89	0
Christian Quarter					
94	0	100	24	64	—
95	0	100	20	71	—
96	0	100	19	46	—
97	0	100	29	65	—
Jewish Quarter					
07	97	3	56	60	17
08	66	34	0?	7	41

* These are the last 2 digits of the official census cell number.

TABLE 9.7. *Occupation and Hebrew language skills*

Occupational group	Speaks	Reads
	%	%
Children 6–16	7	1
Unemployed over 16 (excl. students)	14	4
Students	29	10
Academics, teachers	37	18
Managers, clerks	54	29
Sales, services	57	14
Skilled, semi-skilled	50	9
Unskilled	45	9

and students over the age of 16. But it is the group comprising academics and teachers which is of most interest here, however; for in spite of their high educational level, the academics' Hebrew-speaking ability was lower than all the other employed groups, including the unskilled and the semi-skilled. Their education had not exposed them to Hebrew very much, nor did their work bring them into contact with Hebrew speakers. While workers in the other occupational categories had received less education, they were much more likely to have regular contact with Hebrew speakers, and, as a result, close to half of them was reported to be able to speak Hebrew. Not surprisingly, Hebrew literacy reached its highest level among those Arabs working as clerks.

This tendency for occupation to have an effect on Hebrew-reading and -writing ability can be seen even more clearly if we look at the language skills of those employed in specific occupations (see Table 9.8). As a group, Arab teachers were

TABLE 9.8. *Selected occupations and language skills*

Occupation	Hebrew		English	
	Speak	Read	Speak	Read
	%	%	%	%
Teachers	37	9	89	54
Secretaries	52	29	77	44
Waiters etc.	78	12	60	21
Labourers	41	10	36	10
Drivers	60	13	60	26
Sales/shops	67	19	77	31

generally likely to be able to speak English, but only a third of them was claimed to be able to speak Hebrew. The highest level of Hebrew speaking was found among waiters, followed by people working in shops and by drivers. Note also that 41 per cent of labourers was reported to speak Hebrew, this being the only group, apart from waiters, for which knowledge of Hebrew was reported to be higher than knowledge of English; and that teachers had the lowest level of Hebrew literacy, with secretaries claiming the highest.

These results were confirmed by the follow-up interviews; further information on the learning of Hebrew as a second language is contained in Table 9.9, which looks at the learning environment. It can be seen that only 18 per cent of the Arabs in the second, smaller survey had studied Hebrew at school, but 28 per cent had taken courses in it. All those who had studied Hebrew at school claimed to be able to speak it fluently, and among those claiming to have this ability, 64 per cent said that they learned or practised Hebrew at work, and 28 per cent said that they learned it in the street. Work, then, was clearly the major source of knowledge of Hebrew for this group. Private study was more common among non-speakers (11 per cent) than speakers (3 per cent).

TABLE 9.9. *Where did Arabs say they studied Hebrew?*

	Of those who speak it	Of those who don't	Overall
	%	%	%
School	36	0	18
Courses	42	14	28
Private study	3	11	7
The street	28	6	17
Work	64	8	36
A visit abroad	3	0	1
The media	6	3	4

So, we can say that, among the Arab population, knowledge of Arabic is accounted for by the fact that it is a mother tongue, knowledge of English is mainly related to formal learning, and knowledge of Hebrew is mainly accounted for by informal learning.

Jews' knowledge of Arabic

We have already mentioned that the Jewish population of the Old City has a relatively high level of knowledge of languages, but comparatively few of the Jewish respondents in our sample knew Arabic: just over 17 per cent of those over the age of 9 was reported as being able to carry on a conversation in Arabic, and a bare handful was reported as being literate in Arabic. Arabic was not claimed as a mother tongue by any of the Jews in our sample, a reflection of some bias in our survey and in the socio-economic make-up of the Jewish population of the Old City, which is largely of Ashkenazic background. This low level of knowledge of Arabic may be compared with the high level of knowledge claimed for English, with almost 60 per cent of those Jews in the sample over the age of 9 being reported as knowing it. Some of these were either native speakers or the children of native speakers, but there was a greater correlation between knowledge of English and education than there was between knowledge of English and age; the converse was true of knowledge of Arabic.

The major difference in socio-economic distribution is borne out again by the fact that it is the Jews in academic and liberal professions (the largest group in the sample) who are most likely to know Arabic, whereas it was those Arabs involved in sales, services, and skilled and unskilled labour who were most likely to know Hebrew. One other factor that turned out to have a clear correlation with knowledge of Arabic on the part of Jews over the age of 16 was the length of time they had been in Israel (a correlation of 0.37), confirming that, in this particular sample at least, it was the newer immigrants, presumably those from North Africa and Iraq, who were least likely to know Arabic.

These results were confirmed in the interviews. Since none of the Jews in the smaller sample reported Arabic to be his or her mother tongue, those who did know it must have learned it as a second language. Among those eighteen Jews who claimed to be able to speak Arabic fluently, fifteen learned it in the street, seven had studied it at school, three had taken courses in it, and two had heard it in the home. Many Jews said that they had learned Arabic but were not able to speak it: among this group, a fifth of them had learned it at school, a quarter had taken Arabic courses, a tenth had heard it in the home, and a sixth said that they had picked it up in the street. Work was an insignificant source. One notes that, overall, more than 28 per cent of the Jewish respondents studied Arabic at school (compared to 18 per cent of Arabs who studied Hebrew at school), and 22 per cent had taken courses in it.

10

The Spread of Hebrew among Arabic Speakers

THE fortunes of a language can change as the number of its users and uses expands or contracts. Usually, but not necessarily, the spread of one language occurs at the expense of another. In the Old City we can see at least three examples of language spread: English among all sectors of the population; Hebrew among new immigrants to Israel; and Hebrew among Arabic-speaking residents. The spread of English in Israel (Fishman, Cooper, and Conrad 1977), as well as the spread of Hebrew among the Jewish residents of Palestine and Israel (Cooper 1984), have been described elsewhere. This chapter will examine the spread of Hebrew among Arab residents of the Old City.

The basic issues considered by students of language spread can be collapsed into a single summarizing question (Cooper 1982): who adopts what, when, where, how, and why? This contraction provides us with the framework for this chapter's discussion.

Who?

This question of identity refers to the individual adopters themselves as well as to the communications networks within which they interact. With regard to the former, one wants to establish which characteristics distinguish adopters from non-adopters, and early adopters from late adopters. This is a similar question to one asked by some students of second-language acquisition: what distinguishes good language learners from poor ones? Indeed, language spread and second-language acquisition overlap as fields of enquiry inasmuch as language learning can be viewed as one type of adoption. However, whereas students of second-language acquisition usually study individual differences in attitude, aptitude, cognitive style, learning strategies, and personality, students of language spread usually study demographic characteristics such as age, sex, number of years of formal education, and occupation.

Studies of societal bilingualism have not come up with a universal set of demographic characteristics associated with those who are quick to adopt the spreading language. These studies suggest that if demographic characteristics are related to language spread, it is because they reflect differences in the adopters' incentives and opportunities to learn. For example, Scotton's (1972) study of lingua francas in Kampala found that whereas knowledge of English was related to school attendance, knowledge of Kiswahili was not: the latter can be 'picked up' via the ordinary routines of work, market-place, and neighbourhood, but English is usually learned through formal study. It is hard to do without a knowledge of Kiswahili, but most can manage without a knowledge of English.

What can be learned from the demographic variables associated with Arabs' adoption of Hebrew? The most important determinant of Hebrew acquisition is occupation. Those who encounter and need Hebrew in their work have generally learned it. Education has only a modest influence on the adoption of Hebrew, which appears to be learned primarily outside school. These results are consistent with Singer and Zarbiv's (1989) study of the Arab staff in one of the departments of the Hyatt Hotel in Jerusalem. Most of these men had learned Hebrew, and most of them claimed to have learned it at work. They interact with Jewish colleagues, bosses, and guests in Hebrew. Their work presents them with both the opportunity and the incentive to learn. This seems to be equally true for those of our Arabic-speaking respondents who have learned Hebrew.

As we said at the beginning of this section, the 'who' of our question refers not only to individual adopters but also to the communications networks within which they interact. There is as yet virtually no research directed towards determining which characteristics of communications networks are responsible for promoting or retarding language spread. However, it is plausible that the linguistic heterogeneity of a network will promote the spread of a lingua franca. Indeed, Brosnahan (1963) cites this as one of the four determining conditions in the spread of Greek, Latin, and Arabic throughout their respective empires. Although some residents of the Old City can confine their interactions to those who speak Arabic, this is not possible for all, particularly for those who work with Jews, shop in West Jerusalem, or encounter Jews in the Old City itself. East Jerusalem was linguistically homogeneous during the period of Jordanian occupation from 1948 until 1967, but it is heterogeneous again now. And it is Hebrew not English which has emerged as the main lingua franca between Jews and Arabs, probably because the acquisition of English requires lengthy attendance at school, whereas Hebrew can be acquired informally, and because many Israeli Jews do not know English, whereas almost all of them know Hebrew.

Adopts

Adoption, a notion borrowed from research into the diffusion of innovation, is concerned with the extent to which an innovation has been accepted. Rogers and Shoemaker (1971) suggest that there are five stages to the acceptance of an innovation: awareness (knowledge that the innovation exists), interest (gaining knowledge about an innovation), evaluation (gaining a favourable or unfavourable attitude towards the innovation), small-scale trial, and decision to adopt or reject. Rogers (1983) proposes a somewhat different set of stages: awareness of the innovation's existence, persuasion (gaining a favourable or unfavourable attitude towards it), decision to adopt or reject the innovation, implementation (putting it to use), and confirmation (seeking reinforcement of a previously made decision to adopt the innovation).

My suggestions for the various stages of language spread have been proposed elsewhere (Cooper 1982, 1984): I shall merely summarize them here.

1. Awareness: potential adopters can identify the innovation. During the period of Jordanian occupation it is likely that few Old City residents paid attention to Hebrew. Its salience rose dramatically with the Israeli occupation in 1967.

2. Evaluation: potential adopters form a positive or negative assessment of the personal usefulness of the language. Evaluation here is not the same as favourable or unfavourable feelings towards speakers of the language. English, for example, spread throughout Ireland in spite of Irish antipathy towards the English (Macnamara 1973). Rather, evaluation refers to potential adopters' assessments that knowing or being able to use the new language for a given function will either help or hinder them to attain valued goals. If it will not help them to attain such goals, then the speakers are unlikely to learn it, or, having learned it, they are not likely to use it. 'It is worth remembering', as Whiteley (1969: 13) once remarked, 'that the desire to learn another's language springs only very rarely from a disinterested wish to communicate with one's fellow humans.' Although our survey did not ask the Arabic-speaking respondents questions specifically designed to elicit their attitudes towards learning Hebrew, our impression, based on numerous conversations, is that they take a utilitarian view of the language. They do not seem to feel that learning Hebrew constitutes disloyalty to the Palestinian cause. On the contrary, they believe it will help them to know their adversary as well as to get on in the world of work. It is the latter value, however, which seems to be the chief motivation for learning Hebrew.

3. Proficiency: the speaker is able to use the language for a given function. The criterion of spread here is defined not in terms of grammatical or phonetic accuracy, nor in terms of richness of vocabulary, nor in terms of fluency, but rather in terms of the extent to which speakers can use the language for a given purpose. Knowledge implies the ability to use the language with the right person, at the right time, and at the right place as defined by norms of communicative appropriateness. As we have seen, many more respondents claimed to be able to speak Hebrew than to read it or write it. Presumably, their level of spoken proficiency reflects their contacts at work and in the market-place, the two domains to which Arab use of Hebrew is largely confined.

4. Usage: the speaker uses the language for a given function. Not all who become aware of a language form positive evaluations of its personal usefulness; not all who form positive evaluations learn it; and not all who learn it use it. We

have seen, in fact, that quite a large percentage of the Arabic-speaking respondents with a knowledge of Hebrew report very infrequent use of it.

What?

This question can be approached from two points of view: form and function. Whereas form refers to the structure of the adopted language, function refers to the purposes for which the language is adopted. We will consider function in a later section ('Where?').

The formal characteristics of most concern to students of language spread are, first, the extent to which the spreading language is similar to languages already known by the potential adopter, and, second, the extent to which the spreading language is homogeneous. It is possible that both of these characteristics have promoted Hebrew's spread among Palestinians.

With respect to structural similarity, it seems reasonable to assume that, all things being equal, a language will be adopted more easily if it is similar to one that the potential adopters already know. Thus, one reason commonly advanced for the rapid adoption of Kiswahili is that it spread initially among speakers of other Bantu languages. It is claimed not that similarity is a pre-condition for language spread—the diffusion of Hebrew among Jews who, between them, spoke eighty or ninety different languages provides ample refutation of this claim—but that structural similarity facilitates adoption. Similarity between Arabic and Hebrew has been cited as one reason for the relatively rapid adoption of Hebrew by Arabic-speaking Jews from Asia and Africa, and resemblances between the Ethiopian Semitic languages and Hebrew are likely to have contributed to the relatively rapid acquisition of Hebrew by Ethiopian Jews. It is possible that the similarity between Arabic and Hebrew helped native speakers of the former to learn the latter.

With respect to structural homogeneity, we find, on the one hand, relatively little differentiation in the register used for everyday informal conversation, and, on the other, relatively great differentiation between formal and informal registers. Unlike Palestinian Arabic, which varies from village to village, there is virtually no geographic variation in modern Israeli Hebrew. Differences in terms of social dialects are mainly confined to variations in pronunciation associated with membership of African and Asian ethnic working-class communities. These differences are minimal compared to those to be found in, for example, social-class dialects in England. The relative lack of differentiation in informal Hebrew speech has probably made it easier to learn Hebrew as a second language, and has thus contributed to the speed with which Palestinians have learned the informal vernacular.

If the homogeneity of the informal vernacular has simplified this learning task, the substantial differences between the spoken and written varieties have complicated the task of learning the more 'elevated' varieties of Hebrew. While these differences are not as great as they are in Arabic, they may help to account for the fact that many more of the Arab respondents claimed to be able to speak Hebrew than to read it or write it. (Hebrew and Arabic employ different writing sytems, which probably also contributes to the discrepancy in proficiencies. More important, perhaps, is the fact that the incentive and opportunity to learn to read and write Hebrew is significantly less than the incentive and opportunity to speak it. Jewish immigrants are also less likely to be able to read Hebrew than to speak it: one can manage without reading and writing a language much more easily than one can manage without speaking it.) In short, it is likely that structural homo-geneity has facilitated the spread of vernacular Hebrew among the Palestinians and that structural heterogeneity has contributed to the slower spread of the formal and written varieties.

When?

Time is another variable which has been borrowed from research into the diffusion of innovation. Katz, Levin, and Hamilton (1963) point out that, strictly speaking, it is the period of adoption rather than the adoption itself which is the dependent variable of most interest. Determining this period of adoption means that the characteristics of early and late adopters can be compared, and diffusion curves, showing the number of adopters as a function of time, can be drawn.

While data on the period of adoption are crucial for the study of language spread, they are rarely gathered. This seems to be the case for studies of diffusion generally (Katz, Levin, and Hamilton 1963), probably because of difficulties in obtaining the evidence. Data for Jews suggest that younger immigrants adopt Hebrew more quickly than older immigrants, and that the ability to conduct a simple conversation is the first skill to be acquired, with use of the mass media the last (Rosenbaum 1983). This is likely to be the case for the Arab respondents as well, although we have no data to support this assertion. Singer and Zarbiv's (1989) study of Hyatt Hotel employees suggests that most of the Palestinian workers who learned to speak Hebrew did so within a period of two years. Most of these workers were under 40 years of age.

Where?

This question is concerned with the socially defined location of the interactions through which the language spreads. Thus, location is defined here not in terms of physical or geographical space, but in terms of social space. Fishman's (1964) work on language maintenance and language shift has emphasized the societal domain as a crucial locus for the study of its bilingualism. A domain, according to

Fishman, represents a constellation of social situations which are constrained by the same set of behavioural norms. Examples of domains are those hypothesized for the Puerto Rican speech community of New York: family, neighbourhood, religion, work, and school (Fishman, Cooper, and Ma 1971).

For the Arabic-speaking respondents, the domains associated with the spread of spoken Hebrew appear to be those of work- and market-place. Whereas, among the Jews, the use of Hebrew spread from public to private domains, it is unlikely to spread to private domains among the Palestinians. For the Jews, Hebrew was an *intra*group lingua franca; in other words, those Jews who spoke different mother tongues used Hebrew with one another. For the Palestinians, however, Hebrew is an *inter*group lingua franca, used between Palestinians and Jews. There is no need for a Palestinian intragroup lingua franca, because all Palestinians share the same mother tongue, albeit with local variations.

Our respondents reported little use of Hebrew in bureaucratic encounters, probably because the municipal and state agencies in East Jerusalem employ Palestinian clerks. One type of bureaucratic encounter in which Palestinians do need Hebrew, however, is the filling-out of administrative forms. While these can, in principal, be filled out in Arabic, Palestinians prefer to use Hebrew, probably on the assumption that they will be dealt with more rapidly and favourably. But most Palestinians are incapable of writing Hebrew, and so, outside government buildings in East Jerusalem, there are scribes who, for a fee, will fill out the forms in Hebrew (Adiv 1989).

In what domains have Palestinians acquired the ability to read and write Hebrew? The most likely domain is that of formal education, although a few may have learned informally; for example, a Palestinian student at the Hebrew University told me that his sister taught him the Hebrew alphabet, and that his initial primer consisted of public signs.

How?

How does the potential adopter come to hear about, positively evaluate, learn, and use the spreading language? These questions pertain to the social mechanisms involved in adoption. In the words of Rogers (1983: 17):

the essence of the diffusion process is the information exchange by which one individual Communicates a new idea to one or several others. At its most elementary form, the process involves: (1) an innovation, (2) an individual or other unit of adoption that has knowledge of, or experience with using, the innovation, (3) another individual or unit that does not yet have knowledge of the innovation, and (4) a communication channel connecting the two units. A communication channel is the means by which messages get from one individual to another. The nature of the information exchange relationship between the pair of individuals determines the conditions under which a source will or will not transmit the innovation to the receiver, and the effect of the transfer.

This paradigm, the classic one for the diffusion of innovation, emphasizes the flow of information and persuasion, and the channels of this flow. While this may be appropriate for innovations which must be accepted consciously (e.g. a type of corn, birth-control practices), it seems inappropriate for language spread. None the less, an alternative has yet to be developed. In this connection, investigations into the characteristics of successful language learning may be useful. Although most of these studies have concentrated on psychological factors, some have begun to look at the social strategies that learners employ to learn the language, e.g. the individual with whom learners choose to interact in the target language, and the ways in which they prolong this interaction in order to increase their exposure to the target language.

We did not gather any information on the strategies that our respondents exploited in order to learn Hebrew. Based on unsystematic, informal observation, our impression is that many people are unclear about what they actually did: when asked, they shrug and say they simply 'picked it up'. Participant observation of the type employed by Sorensen (1972) among the Indians of the North-West Amazon, where knowledge of three or four languages is a cultural feature, would probably be necessary in order to find out. Sorensen reports that adults learn a new language by listening to people who speak it, reciting paradigms to themselves, and finally, after a few years, beginning to speak it themselves, but not until they are fairly competent.

In a nation of immigrants it is not surprising, perhaps, that many native speakers have become expert at using a simplified Hebrew for learners. Just as simplified input is thought to help babies learn their first language, so it is likely to help adults learn an additional language. It would be of considerable interest to determine whether the simplified Hebrew addressed to Palestinian workers has the same features as that addressed to new immigrants. Research into 'foreigner' talk suggests that where learners are perceived as belonging to a much lower social class, the simplified speech addressed to them is likely to be more deformed grammatically than if they are perceived as being of an equal or higher status. Perhaps speakers unconsciously employ deformation as a means of barring the learner from full acquisition of the language, and thus from full participation in the community. As yet, we have no documentation of the simplified oral Hebrew addressed either to immigrants or to Palestinians.

Why?

Why do people adopt a new language? As far as Hebrew is concerned, the reasons seem to be the same for Palestinians as they are for new immigrants. Instrumental considerations appear to have been paramount in the adoption of Hebrew by immigrants who arrived after the establishment of the state of Israel. The clear relationship between immigrant participation in the work-force and their adoption of Hebrew bears out the importance of material incentives. Similarly, the relationship between occupational necessity for Hebrew and the acquisition of Hebrew by Palestinians points to the significance of such considerations for them, too. Such an inference is undoubtedly reasonable in view of the importance of material incentives for language spread more generally (Brosnahan 1963; Fishman, Cooper, and Conrad 1977; Cooper 1984). Most of the workers interviewed by Singer and Zarbiv (1989) cited economic considerations as the primary motivation for their acquisition of Hebrew. In general, people learn those languages and those language skills which they need for particular communicative functions. Hebrew will probably continue to spread among Old City Palestinians whilstsoever their participation in the work-force of the Jewish sector goes on growing. Whether the *intifada* will curtail this participation remains to be seen.

11

Conclusions

Urbanization tends to promote both linguistic diversity and uniformity. It promotes diversity inasmuch as occupational specialization and the consequent social stratification are greater in towns than in the countryside, and inasmuch as this social stratification is inevitably reflected by linguistic diversity. Further, towns serve as magnets for migration by speakers of different regional varieties of the same language and by speakers of different languages. At the same time, urbanization promotes uniformity because, working through mass education, it fosters the diffusion of standard languages, and because linguistic diversity gives rise to mediating languages of wider communication.

If standard languages and languages of wider communication serve to unify or provide bridges between diverse urban subgroups, social dialects and ethnic languages serve to maintain and protect the identity of these subgroups, an identity both heightened and threatened by contact between the groups. Thus, the city, with its competing pulls towards uniformity and diversity, provides a fascinating area for socio-linguistic study.

It is not at all surprising that a relatively recent field of enquiry like socio-linguistics should have chosen to focus so much of its attention on a relatively new, but increasingly pervasive, social unit, the city. As I have written elsewhere:

One of the marks of modernism (perhaps its main feature) has been the enormous growth of cities and urban populations throughout the world, a phenomenon that has been even more marked over the last few decades. In 1950, demographers tell us, there were only seven urban centers with more than five million population: now there are 34, and by the year 2025, there could be over 90, 80 of them in emerging nations. (Spolsky 1986b: 172.)

That article also mentioned the linguistic complexity of cities. London was once known as the centre from which Standard English spread: by now it is estimated that fewer than 20 per cent of its schoolchildren speak Standard English. Not so long ago Toronto and Melbourne were considered paradigms of homogeneity and monolingualism; now each is a vibrant example of complex multilingualism, and Melbourne can claim to have the largest Maltese-speaking population of any city in the world, as well as one of the largest concentrations of Greek, Italian, and several other languages. Many of the great urban centres of the world can count their languages in dozens; even such a comparatively tiny site as the Old City shares in this great complexity.

Interest in the socio-linguistics of cities is already a well-established field. Labov's pioneering work in New York (1972) established a methodology and theory for the social stratification of a city as revealed by variations within a single language. Continuing this tradition, such work as that of Trudgill (1974) in Norwich and the Milroys (1978) in Belfast has deepened and enriched our understanding of the way in which social forces and networks shape the patterns of linguistic use and change. With regard to bilingualism, the study conducted by Fishman and his colleagues (Fishman, Cooper, and Ma 1971) into the Jersey City barrio provided us with an important model, suggesting ways of looking in detail at one multilingual part of a larger urban society. The Linguistics Minorities Project (Reid, Smith, and Morawska 1985), a major analysis of the linguistic effects of migration, has plotted the development of multilingualism among a substantial part of the population of London.

Our study has been intended to add to this research, to show how language diversity permits management of urban space, how religious and national diversity are reflected in patterns of language knowledge and use.

In the Introduction we said that our initial motivation for this study was to see how much could be learned about Arab–Jewish relations by looking at the socio-linguistic pattern of the Old City of Jerusalem. The limitations of our research quickly became clear: fascinating though the subject area may be, it is both special, *sui generis*, with unique characteristics that prevent easy generalization, and, at the same time, so closely tied to the rest of the world outside as to provide a more than normally intricate and enigmatic speech community. Other limitations became clear as we used up the time and resources available to us; having finished our comparatively superficial overview, we felt ready to start looking more closely—microscopically even—at the various subcommunities that had been revealed. The initial study whetted our curiosity, and demonstrated how little we had managed to learn.

Nevertheless, we have gleaned a great deal both about the Old City and about the structure of complex multilingual communities. We have learned how a study of signs and of public language use can contribute to an understanding of the various historical, sociological, political, and economic forces that meet in a community. We have seen the constant tension between competing pressures in language choice: the pressure of solidarity that helps to maintain the use of one's own language, and the external proclamation of identity that is inherent in that use even when it might not be understood; the opposing pressure of economic necessity that leads to efforts to learn and use the language of one's customers or employers. We have noted the greater effectiveness of these real-world demands compared with the weaker incentives or encouragements of school language-teaching programmes. Once again we have seen the value of multilingualism in maintaining the identity of variegated communities while providing the opportunity for controlled contact and acculturation.

Our historical digression, which is what it seemed at the time, has provided a valuable background to the present situation, but it has not explained it. In socio-linguistic terms, the Jerusalem of the 1880s was significantly different from the Jerusalem of the 1980s: its official language was that of a distant empire rather than of the contiguous area, so that the vernacular uses of Arabic, Ladino, and Yiddish were unthreatened by Turkish, and the various other European and minority languages were restricted to small communities. The Old City of the 1980s, though now with an Arabic-speaking majority, is sufficiently committed to the dominance of Hebrew outside the walls for that language rapidly to be becoming a necessary second language for all those for whom it is not a mother tongue. The main check on this force is not the learning of Arabic by Hebrew speakers, but the existence of English as a world language, offering an alternative method of communication between Arabs and Jews.

The 1800s represented a period of language change. The rapid increase in the number of Yiddish-speaking Jews was starting to lead to the diffusion of that language among other residents; at the same time, the new immigrants were learning Arabic and starting to incorporate Arabic words and phrases into their Yiddish. The contemporary situation is different; here, the main changes under way appear to be, first, a weakening of the minority languages, as members of the smaller linguistic communities are pulled towards either Arabic or Hebrew; second, a strong, instrumentally driven diffusion of spoken Hebrew into the repertoire of non-native speakers, whether Jewish immigrants or Palestinian residents; and, third, the continued spread of English that is typical of so much of the world today.

So, our historical study provided background for comparison, but it could not explain the contemporary situation because the present population of the Old City is only partly a continuation of the nineteenth-century population, and this means that the political and linguistic events outside the City had their effects there first. The replacement of Turkish rule by British, Jordanian, and then Israeli control had important effects on the Old City; especially significant was the fact that under Turkish, British, and Jordanian rule the infrastructure of the city was allowed to run down, encouraging many former residents (especially the more prosperous) to move outside the walls. The Jews, who made up the majority by 1860, were initially reluctant to move outside the walls, but by the time of the Jordanian occupation there were few of them left to be expelled; many wealthier Arabs moved out, too, to be replaced by squatters from elsewhere.

While the policy of the Israeli government has been to modernize drainage, water, and electricity supplies and to raise the attractiveness of the area considerably, the major rebuilding has been focused on the Jewish quarter, inhabited in the main by people who are not direct descendants of the nineteenth-century population. What we found, therefore, was not historical continuity, but contrast.

As we looked more closely, we found the Old City to be an area not just of linguistic diversity, but one in which linguistic distinctions are constantly reinforced by religious and social differences. Religious and ethnic traditions are strong in the Old City, and residents tend to restrict their social life to mixing with others from the same background and with the same outlook. Even within the religious communities there is evidence of this social cohesion; close social relations are likely to be established only with those from the same synagogue, church, or mosque, or with precisely the same religious and social background. These closed social patterns reinforce language maintenance. Contact with members of other groups is public and not private: Jews and Arabs meet in the street, the shops, the post office, or in a working context, but not socially. It is naïve, then, to imagine that a changed language-teaching policy would lead to changed social relations; only major innovations in social structure, such as common schools or shared military service, could produce the attitudinal basis for such an adjustment.

Nevertheless, there are ways in which changes in language policy could lead to an improvement in relations. The teaching of both spoken and written Arabic in all Jewish schools, and of Hebrew in all Arab schools, would at least provide the basis for communication and for the kind of accommodation sought by the young man at the bus station that we mentioned in the introduction. Knowing another person's language does not make you like them—those Jews who speak Arabic may well be less favourably disposed towards Arabs than those who do not—but it helps mitigate paranoia to have some idea of what other people are saying about you, and knowing something of another person's language enables you to take the first step towards friendship.

In the same way, there could be more sensitivity to the semiotics of public signs. The order of languages on the trilingual street signs, the trilingual sign on Bank Leumi, on the post office, on the Electric Company warning notices, point subtly to the political situation. But the bilingual sign on the police station, without the Arabic which is not only an official language but also the language of most of the residents of the area, carries as negative a message as did the street signs during the Jordanian occupation that omitted Hebrew, testimony to the Jordanian government's banning of Jews—residents, tourists, or pilgrims alike. It is not just informative signs, but symbolic ones, too, that need to respect the languages of the members of the community.

In October and November 1990 the Israel Civil Defence Authority issued gas masks to the civilian population. The flaps of the cardboard boxes are written in Hebrew, but a label has been added to each box explaining that it is not to be opened except in a state of emergency. The label is printed in Hebrew, English, Arabic, and, recognizing the new wave of immigration, in Russian. When the gas masks were given out in the Old City, teams of soldiers were ready to give instruction on their use in Hebrew, English, and Arabic, acknowledging the communicative role of each language.

Ultimately, however, in spite of the importance of language in socialization, the kind of socio-linguistic situation that we have been studying reflects rather than directs social forces. Major changes in the language situation will depend on social and political changes; minor changes in language policy will also follow from, rather than lead to, these social and political changes. Recognizing complexity, and honouring the right to be different—linguistically as well as socially and religiously—is, however, an important basis for social stability in a heterogeneous city. For all its problems, the Old City is a place where that diversity is recognized and respected.

Bibliography

ADIV, GERARD, 1989, 'Filling the Hebrew Reading and Writing Requirements of the Arab Population in East Jerusalem', unpublished seminar paper (in Hebrew), Department of Sociology and Social Anthropology, The Hebrew University of Jerusalem.

ASSAF, M., 1941, *History of the Arabs in Palestine*, ii. *The Arabs under the Crusaders, the Mamelukes and the Turks* (in Hebrew) (Tel Aviv).

AZARYA, VICTOR, 1984, *The Armenian Quarter of Jerusalem* (Berkeley, Calif.).

AZARYAHU (OZRAKOVSKY), JOSEPH, 1910, *Batei hasefer be'eretz Yisrael* [The Schools in Palestine], *Hahinukh* 1/2 (cited in Nahir 1988).

BACHI, R., 1956, 'A Statistical Analysis of the Revival of Hebrew in Israel', *Scripta Hierosolymitana*, 2:179–247.

—— 1977, *The Population of Israel* (Jerusalem).

BACHMAN, L. F., 1990, *Fundamental Considerations in Language Testing* (Oxford).

BAEDEKER, K. (ed.), 1876, *Palestine and Syria: Handbook for Travellers* (Leipzig and London).

BARON, SALO, 1937, *On the History of the Jewish Settlement in Jerusalem* (in Hebrew) (Tel Aviv).

BARTLETT, W. H., 1844, *Walks about the City and Environs of Jerusalem* (London).

—— 1855, *Jerusalem Revisited* (London).

BASILI, R., 1918, *Syrien und Palästina unter der türkischen Regierung* (Odessa).

BEEBE, LESLIE, M. and GILES, HOWARD, 1984, 'Speech-Accommodation Theories: A Discussion in Terms of Second-Language Acquisition', *International Journal of the Sociology of Language*, 46:5–32.

BEN-ARIEH, YEHOSHUA, 1979, *A City Reflected in its Times: New Jerusalem—The Beginnings* (in Hebrew) (Jerusalem).

—— 1984, *Jerusalem in the 19th Century: The Old City* (Jerusalem and New York).

BEN-RAFAEL, ELIEZER, and BROSH, HEZI, 1989, 'A Sociological Study of Second Language Diffusion: The Obstacles to Arabic Teaching in the Israeli Schools', unpublished manuscript.

BENOIT, P., MILIK, J. T., and DE VAUZ, R., 1961, *Les Grottes de Urabba't* (Oxford).

BENTOLILA, Y., 1983, 'The Sociophonology of Hebrew as Spoken in a Rural Settlement of Moroccan Jews in the Negev' (in Hebrew), unpublished doctoral dissertation, The Hebrew University of Jerusalem.

BILMES, J., 1988, 'The Concept of Preference in Conversation Analysis', *Language in Society*, 17: 161–81.

BIRKELAND, H., 1954, *The Language of Jesus* (Oslo).

BLANC, HAIM, 1968, 'The Israeli Koine as an Emergent National Standard', in J. A. Fishman, C. A. Ferguson, and J. Das Gupta (eds.), *Language Problems of Developing Nations* (New York).

BREITBORDE, L. B., 1983, 'Levels of Analysis in Sociolinguistic Explanation: Bilingual

Code Switching, Social Relations, and Domain Theory', *International Journal for the Sociology of Language*, 39: 5–43.

BORSNAHAN, L. F., 1963, 'Some Historical Cases of Language Imposition', in John Spencer (ed.), *Language in Africa* (Cambridge).

CAHANYU, M. N., 1969, *Pray for the Peace of Jerusalem* (in Hebrew) (Jerusalem).

CAPLAN, GERALD, 1980, *Arab and Jew in Jerusalem* (Cambridge, Mass.).

CHOMSKY, WILLIAM, 1957, *Hebrew: The Eternal Language* (Philadelphia).

COHEN-REISS, E., 1967 (2nd edn.), *Memories of a Son of Jerusalem* (in Hebrew) (Jerusalem).

COOPER, ROBERT L., 1968, 'An Elaborated Language Testing Model', *Language Learning*, Special Issue, 3: 57–72.

—— 1982, *Language Spread: Studies in Diffusion and Social Change* (Bloomington, Ind. and Washington, DC).

—— 1984, 'A Framework for the Description of Language Spread: The Case of Modern Hebrew', *International Social Science Journal*, 36/1: 87–112.

—— 1987, 'Planning Language Acquistion', in Peter H. Lowenberg (ed.), *Georgetown University Round Table on Languages and Linguistics 1987* (Washington).

—— 1989, *Language Planning and Social Change* (Cambridge).

—— and CARPENTER, S., 1976, 'Language in the Market', in M. L. Bender, J. D. Bowen, R. L. Cooper and C. A. Ferguson (eds.), *Language in Ethiopia* (London).

—— and FISHMAN, JOSHUA A., 1977, 'A Study of Language Attitudes', *The Bilingual Review* 4/1, 2: 7–34.

—— and GREENBAUM, CHARLES W., 1987, 'Accommodation as a Framework for the Study of Simplified Registers', unpublished manuscript.

CUST, L. G. A., 1929 (repr. 1980 with Hebrew summary), *The Status Quo in the Holy Places* (Jerusalem).

DAOUD, MOHAMED, 1987, 'Arabization in Tunisia: The Tug of War', unpublished seminar paper, Program in Applied Linguistics, University of California at Los Angeles.

DODSON, C. J., 1985, 'Second-Language Acquisition and Bilingual Development: A Theoretical Framework', *Journal of Multilingual and Multicultural Development*, 6/5: 325–46.

DUBNOW, SIMON, 1967, *History of the Jews: From the beginning to Early Christianity*, transl. M. Spiegel (New York).

FAINBERG, YAFFA ALLONY, 1983, 'Linguistic and Sociodemographic Factors Influencing the Acceptance of Hebrew Neologisms'. *International Journal of the Sociology of Language*, 41: 9–40.

FEINSOD-SOKENICK, J., 1929, 'The Development of the Kindergarten', *Hed-hahinukh*, 3: 14–15 (cited in Nahir 1988).

FELDMAN, LOUIS H., 1987, 'How Much Hellenism in Jewish Palestine?', *Hebrew Union College Annual*, 56: 83–111.

FELLMAN, JACK, 1973, 'Concerning the "Revival" of the Hebrew Language', *Anthropological Linguistics*, 15: 250–7.

—— 1974, *The Revival of a Classical Tongue: Eliezer Ben Yehuda and the Modern Hebrew Language* (The Hague).

—— 1977, 'The Hebrew Academy: Orientation and Operation', in Joan Rubin, Bjorn H. Jernudd, Jyotirindra Das Gupta, Joshua A. Fishman, and Charles A. Ferguson (eds.), *Language Planning Processes* (The Hague).

—— and FISHMAN, JOSHUA A., 1977, 'Language Planning in Israel: Solving Terminological Problems', in Joan Rubin, Bjorn H. Jernudd, Jyotirindra Das Gupta, Joshua A. Fishman, and Charles A. Ferguson (eds.), *Language Planning Processes* (The Hague).

FERGUSON, CHARLES E., 1959, 'Diglossia', *Word*, 15: 325–40.

FINN, JAMES, 1878, *Stirring Times, or Records from Jerusalem: Consular Chronicles of 1853–1856*, edited by his widow (London).

FISHMAN, JOSHUA A., 1964, 'Language Maintenance and Language Shift as Fields of Enquiry', *Linguistics*, 9: 32–70.

—— 1971, 'The Relationship between Micro- and Macro-Sociolinguistics in the Study of who Speaks what Language to whom and when', in J. A. Fishman, R. L. Cooper, and R. Ma (eds.), *Bilingualism in the Barrio* (Bloomington, Ind.).

—— 1972, 'Domains and the Relationship between Micro- and Macrosociolinguistics', in John J. Gumperz and Dell Hymes (eds.), *Directions in Sociolinguistics: The Ethnography of Communication* (New York).

—— 1974, 'Language Modernization and Planning in Comparison with Other Types of National Modernization and Planning', in Joshua A. Fishman (ed.), *Advances in Language Planning* (The Hague).

—— 1976, 'Yiddish and Loshn-Koydesh in Traditional Ashkenaz: Problems of Societal Allocation of Macro-Functions', in Albert Verdoodt and Rolf Kjolseth (eds.), *Language in Sociology* (Louvain).

—— 1980, 'Attracting a Following to High-Culture Functions for a Language of Everyday Life: The Role of the Tshernovits Language Conference in the "Rise of Yiddish" ', *International Journal for the Sociology of Language*, 24: 43–73.

—— 1984, 'Mother Tongue Claiming in the United States since 1960: Trends and Correlates Related to the "Revival of Ethnicity" ', *International Journal of the Sociology of Language*, 50: 21–100.

—— COOPER, L., and MA, ROXANA, 1971, *Bilingualism in the Barrio* (Bloomington).

—— —— and CONRAD, A. W., 1977, *The Spread of English: The Sociology of English as an Additional Language* (Rowley, Mass.).

FRAADE, STEVEN, D., 1990, 'Rabbinic Views of the Practice of Targum, and Multilingualism in the Jewish Galilee of the Third–Sixth Centuries', unpublished manuscript.

FREED, B. F., 1980, 'Talking to Foreigners versus Talking to Children: Similarities and Differences', in R. C. Scarcella and S. D. Krashen (eds.), *Research in Second Language Acquisition* (Rowley, Mass.).

FRUMKIN, ABRAHAM, 1940, *In the Springtime of Jewish Socialism* (in Yiddish) (New York).

GENESEE, FRED, 1983, 'Bilingual Education of Majority-Language Children: The Immersion Experiments in Review', *Applied Psycholinguistics*, 4: 1–46.

—— and BOURHIS, RICHARD Y., 1983, 'The Social Psychological Significance of Code Switching in Cross-Cultural Communication', *Journal of Language and Social Psychology*, 1: 1–25.

GERAMB, MARIE-JOSEPH de, 1836, *Pélérinage à Jérusalem et au Mont Sinai en 1831, 1832, et 1833* (Tournay).

—— 1840, *A Pilgrimage to Palestine, Egypt and Syria*, two parts (London).

GLINERT, LEWS, 1987, 'Hebrew–Yiddish Diglossia: Type and Stereotype Implications of the Language of Ganzfried's *Kitzur*', *International Journal of the Sociology of Language*, 67: 39–56.

GOITEIN, S. D., 1971, *A Mediterranean Society: The Jewish Communities of the Arab World as Portrayed in the Documents of the Cairo Geniza*, ii. (*The Community*) (Berkeley, Calif.).

GOLD, DAVID L., 1987, 'Recent Studies in Jewish Languages' (review article), *Language in Society*, 16: 397–408.

GRAETZ, HEINREICH, 1893 (repr. 1967), *History of the Jews*, ii. (New York).

GREENBERG, JOSEPH H., 1966, 'Language Universals', in T. A. Sebeok *et al.* (eds.), *Current Trends in Linguistics*, iii. (The Hague).

GRUNWALD, K., 1975, 'Jewish Schools under Foreign Flags in Ottoman Palestine', in M. Ma'oz (ed.), *Studies on Palestine during the Ottoman period* (Jerusalem).

GUIORA, ALEXANDER Z., and ACTON, WILLIAM R., 1979, 'Personality and Language: A Restatement', *Language Learning*, 29/1: 193–204.

HANY, SUHEIR SHARIF, 1983, 'Language Policy in the Schools of the Old City of Jerusalem, with Particular Reference to English', unpublished MA thesis, The Hebrew University of Jerusalem.

HARTMANN, R., 1910, 'Nebi Musa', *Mitteilungen und Nachrichten des deutschen Palästina-Vereins*, 33: 65–75.

HAVIV (LAUBMAN), D., 1910, 'On Yiddish: A Further Response to Ben-Yehuda, *Ha'or*, 1: 128 (cited in Nahir 1988).

HAZIKHRONI, 1902, Letter to the editor, *Hashkafa*, 3: 32. (cited in Nahir 1988).

HENGEL, MARTIN, 1974, *Judaism and Hellenism* (London).

HOFMAN, J., and FISHERMAN, H., 1971, 'Language Shift and Language Maintenance in Israel', *International Migration Review*, 5: 204–26.

HYAMSON, ALBERT M. (ed.), 1939, 1941. *The British Consulate in Jerusalem in Relation to the Jews of Palestine 1838–1914*, i. *1838–1861*; ii. *1862–1914* (London).

KAIMIO, J., 1979, *The Romans and the Greek Language*, Societas Scentiarum Fennica, Commentationes Humanarum Litterarum 64 (Helsinki).

KAMINICER, MENACHEM-MENDEL, 1839 (repr. 1975), *Sefer Korot Ha'ittim* (Vilna and Jerusalem).

KATZ, ELIHU, LEVIN, MARTIN L., and HAMILTON, HERBERT, 1963, 'Traditions of Research on the Diffusion of Innovation', *American Sociological Review*, 28: 237–52.

KATZOFF, RANON, 1980, 'Sources of Law in Roman Egypt: The Role of the Prefect', *Aufstieg und Niedergang der römischen Welt*, 2/13: 807–44.

KLAUSNER, J., 1915, *Olam mit-haveh* [A World Being Formed] (cited in Nahir 1988) (Odessa).

KLOSS, HEINZ, 1966, 'German–American Language Maintenance Efforts', in Joshua A. Fishman (ed.), *Language Loyalty in the United States* (The Hague).

—— 1968, 'Notes Concerning a Language–Nation Typology', in J. A. Fishman, C. A. Ferguson, and J. Das Gupta (eds.), *Language Problems of Developing Nations* (New York).

—— 1969, *Research Possibilities on Group Bilingualism: A Report* (Quebec).

KOSOVER, MORDECAI, 1966, *Arabic Elements in Palestinian Yiddish: The Old Ashkenazic Jewish Community in Palestine—its History and its Language* (Jersualem).

LABOV, WILLIAM, 1972, *Sociolinguistic Patterns* (Philadelphia).

LEVINE, LEE I., 1975, *Caesarea under Roman Rule* (Leiden).

LEWIS, E. GLYN, 1972, *Multilingualism in the Soviet Union* (The Hague).

LIEBERMAN, SAUL, 1942, *Greek in Jewish Palestine* (New York).

—— 1950, *Hellenism in Jewish Palestine* (New York).

LOEWE, L. (ed.), 1890, *Diary of Sir Moses and Lady Montefiore* (London).

LUNCZ, A. M., 1882–1919, *Jerusalem Yearbook for the Diffusion of an Accurate Knowledge of Ancient and Modern Palestine* (in Hebrew), 13 vols. (Jerusalem).

MACNAMARA, JOHN, 1973, 'Attitudes and Learning a Second Language', in Roger W. Shuy and Ralph W. Fasold (eds.), *Language Attitudes: Current Trends and Prospects* (Washington, DC).

MEYERS, ERIC M., and STRANGE, JAMES F., 1981, *Archaeology, the Rabbis, and early Christianity* (Abingdon, Nash.).

MILROY, J., and MILROY, L., 1978, 'Belfast: Change and Variation in an Urban Vernacular,' in P. Trudgill (ed.), *Sociolinguistic Patterns in British English* (London).

MÜHLHÄUSLER, PETER, 1988, 'Towards an Atlas of the Pidgins and Creoles of the Pacific Area', *International Journal of the Sociology of Language*, 71: 37–49.

NAHIR, MOSHE, 1988, 'Language Planning and Language Acquisition: The "Great Leap" in the Hebrew Revival', in C. B. Paulston (ed.), *International Handbook of Bilingualism and Bilingual Education* (New York).

NEUMANN, B., 1877, *Die Heilige Stadt und deren Bewohner* (Hamburg).

ORELLI, G., 1868, Durch's Leilige Land (cited in Ben-Arieh 1984) (Basel).

PARFITT, T. V., 1972, 'The Use of Hebrew in Palestine 1800–1882', *Journal of Semitic Studies*, 42/2: 237–52.

PATTERSON, DAVID, 1989, 'Assimilation and Acculturation as Reflected in Hebrew Literature in Czarist Russia', paper read at the International Symposium on Assimilation and Acculturation, Bar-Ilan University, 28 December 1989—1 January 1990.

PETERMANN, I., 1860–1, *Reisen im Orient* (Leipzig).

PETROZZI, M. T., 1971, 'The Franciscan Printing Press', *Christian News from Israel*, 22: 64–9.

PFEIFFER, ROBERT H., 1949, *History of New Testament Times* (New York).

PILOWSKY, ARYE L., 1985, 'Yiddish alongside the Revival of Hebrew: Public Polemics on the Status of Yiddish in Eretz Israel, 1907–1929', in Joshua A. Fishman (ed.), *Readings in the Sociology of Jewish Languages* (Leiden).

PIRHI, J., 1905, 'A Question to the Founders of the Kindergarten', *Hashkafa*, 6: 21 (cited in Nahir 1988).

PRAWER, JOSHUA, 1972, *The World of the Crusaders* (London).

PRESS, J., 1921, *Eretz-Israel and South Syrian Travel Handbook* (in Hebrew) (Jerusalem).

PROGES (PREGER), MOSES, 1650, *Darke Zion* [An Itinerary of Palestine] (cited by Kosover 1966) (Prague?).

RABIN, CHAIM, 1958, 'The Historical Background of Qumran Hebrew'. *Scripta Hierosolymita*, 4: 144–61.

—— 1973, *A Short History of the Jewish Language* (Jerusalem).

—— 1975, 'The Ancient and the Modern: Ancient Source Materials in Present-Day Jewish Writing', in H. Paper (ed.), *Language and Text: The Nature of Linguistic Evidence* (Ann Arbor).

—— 1976, 'Hebrew and Aramaic in the First Century', *Compendia Rerum Iudicarium ad Novum Testamentum*, ii. (Assen).

—— 1981, 'What Constitutes a Jewish Language?', *International Journal of the Sociology of Language*, 30: 19–28.

—— 1983, 'The Sociology of Normativism in Israeli Hebrew', *International Journal of the Sociology of Hebrew*, 41: 41–56.

REID, EUAN, SMITH, GREG, and MORAWSKA, ANNA, 1985, *Languages in London* (London).

REICHER, M., 1870, *The Gates of Jerusalem* (in Hebrew) (Lemberg).

RITTER, CARL, 1866, *The Comparative Geography of Palestine and the Sinaitic Peninsula*, trans. and adapted by W. L. Gage, 4 vols. (Edinburgh).

ROBINSON, EDWARD (ed.), 1841, *Biblical Researches in Palestine, Mount Sinai and Arabia Petraea: A Journal of Travels in the Year 1838 by E. Robinson and E. Smith*, 3 parts (London).

ROGERS, EVERETT M., 1983 (3rd ed.), *Diffusion of Innovations* (New York).

—— and SHOEMAKER, F. FLOYD, 1971 (2nd edn), *Communication of Innovations: A Cross-Cultural Approach* (New York).

ROSENBAUM, Y., 1983, 'Hebrew Adoption among New Immigrants to Israel: The First Three Years', *International Journal of the Sociology of Language*, 41: 115–30.

—— NADEL, E., COOPER, R. L., and FISHMAN, J. A., 1977, 'English on Keren Kayemet Street', in J. A. Fishman, R. L. Cooper and A. W. Conrad (eds.), *The Spread of English: The Sociology of English as an Additional Language* (Rowley, Mass.).

RUBIN, JOAN, 1977, 'Language Standardization in Indonesia', in Joan Rubin, Bjorn H. Jernudd, Jyotirindra Das Gupta, Joshua A. Fishman, and Charles A. Ferguson (eds.), *Language Planning Processes* (The Hague).

SAFRAI, S., 1975, 'The Temple and the Divine Service', in Michael Avi-Yonah and Zvi Baras (eds.), *The Herodian Period*, vol. 7 of *The World History of the Jewish People* (New Brunswick).

SCHMELZ, U. O., and BACHI, R., 1974, 'Hebrew as an Everyday Language of the Jews in Israel: A Statistical Appraisal', in American Academy for Jewish Research, *Salo Wittmayer Baron Jubilee Volume*, ii. (New York).

SCHWARTZ, J. 1845 (3rd rev. edn. 1900), *The Produce of the Land* (in Hebrew) (Jerusalem); English trans. by Isaac Leeser, Philadelphia, 1850).

SCOTTON, CAROL MYERS, 1972, *Choosing a Lingua Franca in an African Capital* (Edmonton and Champaign).

—— 1983, 'The Negotiation of Identities in Conversation: A Theory of Markedness and Code Choice', *International Journal of the Sociology of Language*, 44: 116–36.

SEETZEN, U. J., 1854–9, *Reisen durch Syrien, Palaestina* (Berlin).

SEGAL, MOSES H., 1908, 'Mishnaic Hebrew and its Relation to Biblical Hebrew and to Aramaic', *Jewish Quarterly Review*, 20: 647, 737.

—— 1927, *A Grammar of Mishnaic Hebrew* (Oxford).

SEMYATITSHER, GEDALYA, 1716 (rev. edn. 1927), *Shaalu Shelom Yerushalaim* [On the Situation of the Ashkenazic Community in Jerusalem at the Beginning of the Eighteenth Century] (Berlin; 2nd edn., with introduction and notes by Z. Rubashov, in *Reshumoth*, 2: 462–93, cited by Kosover 1966).

SHARVIT, SHIMON, 1980, 'The Tense System of Mishnaic Hebrew' (in Hebrew), in G. B. Safartti *et al.* (eds.), *Studies in Hebrew and Semitic Languages, Dedicated to the Memory of Professor Eduard Yechezkel Kutscher* (Ramat-Gan).

SINGER, RONEN, and ZARBIV, SAMI, 1989, 'The Hebrew Proficiency of Some Arab Workers at the Hyatt Hotel', unpublished seminar paper (in Hebrew), Department of Sociology and Social Anthropology, The Hebrew University of Jerusalem.

SMILANSKY, ZE'EV, 1930, *Letoldot hadibur ha'ivri be'eretz yisrael* [Towards a History of Spoken Hebrew in Palestine], *Hapo'el Hatsa'ir*, 23: 7 (cited in Nahir 1988).

SNOW, C. E., VAN EEDEN, R., and MUYSKEN, P., 1981, 'The Interactional Origins of Foreigner Talk: Municipal Employees and Foreign Workers', *International Journal of the Sociology of Language*, 28: 411–30.

SORENSEN, A. P., JR., 1972, 'Multilingualism in the Northwest Amazon', in J. B. Pride and Janet Holmes (eds.), *Sociolinguistics: Selected Readings* (Harmondsworth; rev. version of 'Multilingualism in the Northwest Amazon', *American Anthropologist*, 69 (1967), 670–84.

SPOLSKY, BERNARD, 1983, 'Triglossia and Literacy in Jewish Palestine of the First Century'. *International Journal for the Sociology of Language*, 42: 95–110.

—— 1985, 'Jewish multilingualism in the First Century: An Essay in Historical Socio-linguistics', in Joshua A. Fishman (ed.), *Readings in the Sociology of Jewish Languages* (Leiden).

—— 1986*a*, 'Avoiding the Tyranny of the Written Word: The Development of the Mediated Mode of Jewish Literacy from the First to Tenth Centuries', *Australian Review of Applied Linguistics*, 9/2: 23–37.

—— 1986*b*, 'Overcoming Language Barriers to Education in a Multilingual World', in B. Spolsky (ed.), *Language and Education in Multilingual Settings* (Clevedon).

—— 1989, *Conditions for Second Language Learning: Introduction to a General Theory* (Oxford).

—— and HOLM, WAYNE, 1971, 'Literacy in the Vernacular: The Case of Navajo', United States Bureau of Indian Affairs, *Curriculum Bulletin*, 3: 59–65; repr. in Ralph W. Ewton, Jr., and Jacob Ornstein (eds.), *Studies in language and linguistics, 1972–3* (El Paso).

STEWART, R. W., 1857, *The Tent and Khan: A Journey in Sinai and Palestine* (London).

STRAUSS, F. A., 1947, *Sinai und Golgotha: Reise in das Morgenland* (Berlin).

STREET, R. R., JR., and GILES, H., 1982, 'Speech Accommodation Theory: A Social Cognitive Approach to Language and Speech Behavior', in M. Roloff and C. Berger (eds.), *Social Cognition and Communication* (Beverly Hills, Calif.).

STREVENS, P. D., 1978, 'The Nature of Language Teaching', in J. Richards (ed.), *Understanding Second and Foreign Language Learning* (Rowley, Mass.).

TAYLOR, I. J. S., 1855, *La Syrie, la Palestine, et al Judée* (Paris).

TCHERIKOVER, VICTOR, and FUKS, ALEXANDER, 1957, *Corpus papyrorum Judaicarum* (Cambridge, Mass.).

TIBAWI, A. L., 1972, *Islamic Education, its Tradition and Modernizations in the Arab National System* (London).

TOBLER, T., 1853, *Denkblatter aus Jerusalem* (Constance).

TRUDGILL, PETER, 1974, *The Social Differentiation of English in Norwich* (Cambridge).

WARREN, CHARLES, 1876, *Underground Jerusalem: An Accouont of Some of the Principal Difficulties Encountered in its Exploration and the Results Obtained* (London).

WEBBER, JONATHAN, 1979, 'The Status of English as a *Lingua Franca* in Contemporary Jerusalem', D. Phil. thesis, 2 vols. (Oxford).

WEINREICH, MAX, 1980, *History of the Yiddish Language*, trans. S. Noble and J. A. Fishman (Chicago).

WHITELEY, WILFRED H., 1969, *Swahili: the Rise of a National Language*, Studies in African History 3 (London).

WIGODER, G., 1972, 'Israel, State of (Cultural Life)', *Encyclopedia Judaica*, ix. (Jerusalem).

WILSON, C. W., 1866, *Ordnance Survey of Jerusalem Made in the Years 1864 to 1865* (Southampton).

WILSON, J., 1847, *The Lands of the Bible Visited and Described* (London).

YELLIN, D., 1972, *The Writings of David Yellin*, i. *The Jerusalem of Yesterday* (in Hebrew) (Jerusalem).

Index